HOW TO STOP A CONSPIRACY

ANCIENT WISDOM FOR MODERN READERS

■ ■ ■ ■ ■

For a full list of titles in the series, go to https://press.princeton
.edu/series/ancient-wisdom-for-modern-readers.

HOW TO STOP A CONSPIRACY

■ ■ ■ ■ ■ ■

An Ancient Guide to Saving a Republic

Sallust

Translated and introduced
by Josiah Osgood

PRINCETON UNIVERSITY PRESS

PRINCETON AND OXFORD

Published by Princeton University Press
41 William Street, Princeton, New Jersey 08540
99 Banbury Road, Oxford OX2 6JX

press.princeton.edu

All Rights Reserved
ISBN 9780691212364
ISBN (e-book) 9780691229584

British Library Cataloging-in-Publication Data is available

Editorial: Rob Tempio, Matt Rohal, and Chloe Coy
Production Editorial: Mark Bellis
Text and Jacket Design: Pamela L. Schnitter
Production: Erin Suydam
Publicity: James Schneider and Carmen Jimenez
Copyeditor: Cynthia Buck

Jacket Credit: From Cesare Maccari, *Cicero in the Roman Senate,
Accusing Catiline*, 1880, fresco / Alamy Stock Photo

This book has been composed in Stempel Garamond

Printed on acid-free paper. ∞

Printed in the United States of America

1 3 5 7 9 10 8 6 4 2

CONTENTS

INTRODUCTION

> You go on, I presume, with your Latin
> Exercises: and I wish to hear of your
> beginning upon Sallust who is one of the
> most polished and perfect of the Roman
> Historians, every Period of whom, and
> I had almost said every Syllable and
> every Letter is worth Studying.
>
> —JOHN ADAMS TO JOHN QUINCY ADAMS, 1781

Fears of conspiracy were widespread among the
founders of the United States. Members of the
British government, it was claimed, were secretly scheming to rob Americans of all their
liberties. Much of the Declaration of Indepen-
dence itself outlines a plot by King George III
to establish "an absolute tyranny over these
states."

And ever since the Revolutionary War, the
historian Richard Hofstadter famously argued,
American political life has often witnessed a

"paranoid style" marked by "heated exaggeration."[1] Nineteenth-century nativists, Hofstadter pointed out, denounced Catholic plots against America with invented details of "libertine priests" and "licentious convents."[2] Abolitionists thundered about the conspiracy of slaveholders, the so-called Slave Power. And more recently, Donald Trump's election in 2016 was accompanied by allegations that his campaign had colluded with Wikileaks and Russia. Trump, in turn, claimed that it was Ukraine that intervened, on behalf of the Democrats. He and his supporters railed endlessly about the "Deep State" plot against him—and some embraced QAnon, a strange theory centered on a cabal of Satan-worshiping pedophiles.

While stories about shadowy plots might often seem deranged, they can also be perfectly rational. In an important reconsideration of conspiratorial thinking in the era of the American Revolution, Gordon Wood has argued that conspiracy theories, which were actually widespread in the eighteenth century, reflected the Enlightenment effort to explain the world clearly—to attribute events not to the will of God, but to the deep, sometimes hidden, passions of

men.[3] In political situations of increasing complexity, Wood suggested, conspiracy accounted for developments that otherwise seemed unpredictable. This is a powerful interpretation that, though rooted in the eighteenth century, can provide insights into conspiracy narratives of more recent times.

And of course, as Hofstadter himself pointed out, "there *are* conspiratorial acts in history, and there is nothing paranoid about taking note of them."[4] John Wilkes Booth led a successful conspiracy against Abraham Lincoln, just as two millennia earlier a group of secret plotters assassinated Julius Caesar on the Ides of March, 44 BC. Trump's presidency itself culminated with an all too real attack on the US Capitol, parts of which were planned well in advance.

One especially powerful exploration of conspiracy—including the problem of distinguishing between claims of conspiracy and the real thing—is a short book written in the late 40s BC, Sallust's *The War against Catiline*. The first foray of Sallust into history-writing, *The War against Catiline* recounts a plot by the corrupt aristocrat Lucius Sergius Catilina (known in English as "Catiline") to topple the Republic in

the year 63 BC. As alluring as he was dangerous, Catiline attracted a wide array of supporters: men and women from prominent families
who had run up debts; impressionable youths
eager for sex, money, or other favors; and the im-
poverished inhabitants of Rome fed up with a
political class that seemed only to look out for
its own interests. Frustrated in his efforts to win
election to the top office of consul, Catiline fled
Rome and joined up with his forces in northern
Italy while several of his associates stayed behind
with secret plans to torch the city and murder
its leading politicians. *The War against Catiline*
powerfully culminates with the unmasking of
these urban conspirators at a meeting of the Senate, followed by a stormy debate that led to their
immediate execution and then the ultimate defeat
of Catiline and his two legions in battle.

At the heart of Sallust's story is the mesmer-
izing figure of Catiline, a bitter and haunted
man who was bent on gaining dominance over
the state, yet sympathetic to the plight of struggling Romans. Sallust powerfully describes the
violent commotions within Catiline's mind and
the way they could be seen in his pale complex-
ion, his bloodshot eyes, "his step now quick,

now slow." So strong was the disturbance within him that it could not be contained. It spilled out and engulfed the whole Republic.

Along with Catiline, some of the most important figures of Roman history make memorable appearances. We see Cicero, the ambitious politician who held the consulship in 63, calculating how best to protect Rome. We see Julius Caesar, the future dictator, fingered in the conspiracy by his enemies. Sallust, who fought for Caesar in the great civil war that broke out in 49 and quickly engulfed the whole Mediterranean world, absolves him of any complicity. In re-creating the debate that took place on the punishment of the conspirators, Sallust has Caesar give a long and principled speech arguing against summary execution. We then hear the man destined to become Caesar's most dangerous rival, Cato the Younger, give a stern rejoinder highlighting the danger of not taking swift action. Quite unexpectedly, Sallust concludes his account of the debate by remarking that while Cato and Caesar had utterly different characters, they were the two great men of their time.

The age was one in which almost every politician, according to Sallust, cared nothing for

the common good and fought only to uphold his own power. Public life had been tainted by a long civil war in the 80s that ended with the victory of the unscrupulous general Sulla. Not only had Sulla seized power by force and dangerously indulged the army that fought for him, but after establishing himself in Rome he had issued long lists of citizens he wished to outlaw, the so-called proscriptions. Rewards were offered to anyone who killed the proscribed, their property was confiscated, and their sons and grandsons were banned from holding public office. Sulla's minions started adding names to the proscription list just to secure a fine house or villa or even a work of art. Soon, as Sallust puts it, "everyone was plundering and robbing." Wealth became the major source of honor in Rome, and "was accompanied by glory, power, and influence." Sallust was fascinated by Catiline in part because the corrupt aristocrat seemed the perfect embodiment of this new rapacity and ruthlessness.

The War against Catiline has much to offer readers today. In it, Sallust offers an account of the conspiracy that influenced how later classically educated Europeans and Americans saw

their world.[5] He includes jaw-dropping details, while also foregrounding the common problem of separating fact from fiction in shadowy reports about a conspiracy. In addition, Sallust offers a warning of what happens when a society's leaders see politics only as a source of personal power and neglect pressing social problems that may predispose individuals to take actions harmful to public order. In Sallust's view, a republic's success is tied directly to the willingness of its people to put it ahead of themselves. The alarming story he tells challenges us to think about the difference between good and bad leadership, and about our individual ability to affect our culture and politics for better or worse.

How to Stop a Conspiracy

At the heart of conspiracy lies a paradox. Since a conspiracy is a secret plot, the more successful it is, the less evidence there will be for it. At the outermost extreme, a complete absence of evidence may be a sign that a particularly diabolical conspiracy has taken place. It is precisely this paradox, of course, that conspiracy theorists

exploit. But a corollary of this possibility is that it may be hard to get anyone to believe that a conspiracy is afoot. As the emperor Domitian—admittedly, one of the most suspicious men ever to hold power in Rome—liked to complain: no one believes in a plot against an emperor until it has succeeded.[6]

As consul in the year 63, Cicero faced a variation on this problem. Catiline, born around 108, belonged to one of the small number of Rome's patrician families who traced their ancestry back to the earliest days of the city, but the family's fortunes had decayed. No member of it had held the consulship for generations—a deficit Catiline was determined to overcome. About twenty-five years old when Sulla marched victorious into Rome, Catiline killed at least several men during the proscriptions, and an air of scandal hung about him afterwards. In the year 73, for instance, he was accused of having sex with a Vestal Virgin—a serious offense punishable by death. Catiline escaped conviction with help from one of his powerful friends, a fellow aristocrat who had also supported Sulla.

Catiline first ran for the consulship in 64. Two consuls were elected each year, and Catiline

hoped to serve alongside Gaius Antonius, a brutal man who had been a loyal officer under Sulla and was another of Catiline's friends. While Antonius did secure one of the two consulships for 63, Catiline did not. To add to the patrician's humiliation, he was beaten out by Cicero, a so-called new man, the first in his family to enter the Senate. When a second chance came the next year, the stakes were even higher. Catiline, who had always lived profligately, was apparently on the verge of bankruptcy. Without the consulship and the lucrative provincial governorship that would follow from it, he might be ruined.

Modern historians have sometimes argued— against the testimony of Cicero, Sallust, and other ancient writers—that Catiline only entered on conspiracy after his second defeat in 63.[7] But a careful study of chronology strongly suggests that even before the election he was making plans to seize the consulship by force if he failed in the polls.[8]

As Catiline well knew, Italy was now in the grip of a full-scale debt crisis. Debt levels were chronically high, but in 63 there was a particular problem: after years of instability, peaceful conditions had finally been restored to the

Roman East, and financiers were calling in loans they had placed in Italy so that they could reinvest their capital at even higher rates of interest abroad. Already at the start of 63 there were calls for a onetime cancellation of debts, and Catiline now made debt relief the platform of his consular campaign. New supporters flocked to Catiline—not just fellow senators in debt, but also the urban poor, who struggled to pay the rents on the rickety apartments they lived in, and small-scale farmers in the Italian countryside. The most powerful allies Catiline found were a group of especially desperate men in northern Italy who were being organized into an unofficial army by an old officer under Sulla named Manlius. From these supporters Catiline might win some votes—indeed, Manlius and his men came to Rome to support Catiline's election. But if, as seemed increasingly possible, Catiline lost, he could use them to march on Rome, remove Cicero (and perhaps Antonius too), and seize power for himself and his supporters.

One of the pleasures of reading *The War against Catiline* lies in the account of how Cicero thwarted Catiline's plans. We learn something

that Cicero never revealed in the speeches he gave denouncing Catiline—that the mistress of an especially foolish senator who supported Catiline was Cicero's main source of information. And after Catiline himself left Rome in early November 63, we see Cicero intriguing to secure written evidence that would prove the guilt of the high-ranking associates whom Catiline had left behind in the city. At a dramatic meeting of the Senate on December 3, 63, Cicero unsealed the documents and confronted the conspirators with them. It was the equivalent of the "smoking gun" tape that brought down President Richard Nixon.

One part of stopping a conspiracy, Sallust shows, is to launch a counterconspiracy. As the conspirator plots secretly, his opponent must do the same; the opponent must cultivate secret informants, covertly gathering evidence and sharing it only when it becomes overwhelming. Another paradox of conspiracies is that those trying to thwart one might need to bend or even break the law themselves in the higher interest of saving the state. Sallust suggests that the swift execution of the conspirators in Rome not only spared the city turmoil but also

led many in Catiline's army in northern Italy to defect. Cato's recommendation for immediate punishment without a trial thus seems to have been expedient in the short term, though Caesar's speech leaves us with questions about the long-term consequences of such a decision.

While recognizing Cicero's guile, Sallust draws even more attention to how hard it was to obtain information on the conspiracy and to get citizens to view it as a real threat. Even though the Senate offered large cash rewards for information, nobody came forward. And many ordinary citizens still supported Catiline, as Sallust laments, even after he had fled to Manlius's camp and illegally assumed the trappings of consular office. The Senate itself long hesitated over taking any action against him, owing in part to a lack of hard evidence. But for Sallust, that Catiline got as far along in his plans as he did was a sign of the overall corruption in Rome. Despite conquering the known world, the historian writes, the Romans were shockingly weak, committed to upholding only their own individual interests. After Sulla, politicians seemed bent on ruining the Republic.

INTRODUCTION

Sallust and the Struggle for Power

Sallust found the corruption of Rome, and of Rome's politicians in particular, an appealing topic for personal reasons. Born in 86 in the town of Amiternum, about fifty miles northeast of Rome, Sallust was, like Cicero, a new man. His family must have been wealthy, however, since as a youth he decided to pursue a career in politics—an impossible undertaking in Rome for those without substantial means. Nothing is known of how he got his start, but by 52— about ten years before he started writing *The War against Catiline*—he was serving in the office of the tribune of the plebs. Ten tribunes were elected annually, and by tradition they were supposed to represent the interests of ordinary citizens, the plebs. Tribunes could propose legislation to one of the main popular assemblies, and they also enjoyed the right to summon public meetings in the Forum, the great public square in the heart of Rome. Up onto the lofty Speaker's Platform they would climb to address crowds that might number several thousand.

It was a turbulent time to be a tribune. The year 52 opened with no senior magistrates in office after the suspension of elections in the previous year because of fighting in the streets of Rome. Then, on January 18, one of the candidates who had been seeking office, the great popular champion Clodius, was murdered by a rival on the Appian Way just outside the city. His body was brought back to Rome and displayed in the Forum. In their anger and grief, the people carried Clodius's body into the Senate-house, made a pyre of the benches there, and then burned the body along with the Senate-house itself. Along with two other tribunes, Sallust took the lead in denouncing Clodius's murderer and demanding punishment.

As Sallust explains in *The War against Catiline*, there were two familiar types of politicians in his day. One sort, well represented by Clodius, saw power as firmly residing in the Republic's popular assemblies and sought to pass legislation there that would uphold the people's interests—for instance, laws distributing grain at a subsidized price or for free. The other sort preferred an older tradition of letting the Senate manage affairs, especially finance and foreign

policy. The Senate was made up of five hundred to six hundred men who customarily held membership for life, after they were elected to their first magistracy. And by tradition, its deliberations were guided by the senior magistrates and ex-magistrates, most of whom belonged to "the nobility"—a relatively small number of families who enjoyed electoral success generation after generation. For both these reasons, the champions of senatorial dominance were often quite conservative, convinced that only they knew what was right for Rome. They sometimes identified themselves as the *optimates* ("the best men") or the *boni* ("the good men").

In the year of his tribunate, Sallust clearly acted as a popular politician. And there are many hints throughout his historical writings of sympathy for the popular viewpoint. Sallust never uses the flattering term *optimates*, for instance. He prefers to write scathingly of the power of the "few." Also, the utterly hostile picture of Sulla that emerges in *The War against Catiline* was in keeping with popular views. After his victory in the civil war, Sulla tried to prop up the traditional dominance of the nobles and actually passed legislation to strip the tribunes of

much of their power, hoping that this would curtail popular politics. But the people grew increasingly unhappy, and about a decade later tribunician power was fully restored when Gnaeus Pompeius ("Pompey" in English) and Marcus Licinius Crassus—two of the most powerful politicians of the era—shared the consulship in 70.

Yet of the new crop of popular politicians that now sprang up, Sallust has little good to say. In stirring up citizens with their attacks on the Senate, Sallust believes, these politicians, like the *optimates*, were really only trying to advance their own interests. In a deeply pessimistic verdict, Sallust concludes that, for all the honorable pretexts of "defending the rights of people" or "keeping the influence of the Senate supreme," the politics of his day was at heart a naked struggle for individual power. Everyone claimed to be acting for the "common good"; nobody actually cared about it.

Sallust turned to history in disappointment and despair. Two years after his tribunate, he was expelled from the Senate. It was then that he attached himself to Caesar and served on Caesar's military staff during the civil war that

broke out in 49. He regained membership in the Senate and then distinguished himself on a campaign in Africa. As a reward, Caesar made him the first governor of a new province created there. But according to the later historian Cassius Dio, Sallust pillaged the province and escaped conviction for embezzlement only by the personal intervention of Caesar.[9] It was another disgrace. Probably at that point, or perhaps after Caesar's murder on the Ides of March in 44, when civil war started to flare up again, Sallust decided to withdraw from politics altogether.[10]

History provided Sallust with a chance to redeem himself. In exposing the politics of his day as nothing more than a squalid struggle for power, he was justifying his withdrawal from it. By Sallust's account, because only money seemed to matter now, politicians would do anything to get ahead. They stole from provincials. They stripped temples of their wealth. They even killed each other in civil war. Values became perverted: poverty was now considered a disgrace, virtue a weakness, integrity a form of nastiness to others. Sallust proudly told his readers that he was leaving it all behind and instead

would offer an explanation of how this state of affairs had come to pass.

Earlier Roman historical writing was often heavily patriotic, and its approach was ill suited to exploring the political crisis of Sallust's day. For inspiration, he turned to the greatest of Greek historians, Thucydides. In his history of the thirty-year-long Peloponnesian War between Athens and Sparta, Thucydides had pioneered a new realism. Removing the gods as the explanation for human prosperity and suffering, Thucydides insisted on peering closely at men and states themselves, to see how they actually behaved. He was fascinated by the gap between the honorable pretexts that human beings held out for their actions and the cold fact that most acted out of self-interest, especially under the pressure of war or political crisis. At such times, he showed, a society's political, social, and religious mores could quickly break down. "Fair phrases" would give cover "to those who would carry through odious deeds."[11]

Sallust clearly found Thucydides's descriptions of wars and politics applicable to his own times and evoked them. He even tries to re-create,

in Latin, the blunt, often harsh, style of Thucydides's Greek. To shock readers into seeing reality, Sallust favors abrupt pronouncements, surprising vocabulary, and words arranged in an unexpected order or combined in unexpected ways. He rejects the modern elegance of Ciceronian prose and deliberately revives archaic meanings of words and even archaic spellings (an effect I have not tried to capture in this translation).

A particular attraction for Sallust of Thucydides was his interest in the rise and fall of states. Thucydides's *History* not only has as its subject the ruin of the Athenian empire but begins with an "archaeology" in which Thucydides tries to piece together the earliest history of the Greek world. States grew powerful, the historian theorizes, through the acquisition of wealth, which allowed them to fund navies with which they could dominate other peoples and so raise more money. Such a theory, however, could not really account for the growth of Roman power, nor could it explain Rome's descent into the nasty civil wars of Sallust's day. Emulating Thucydides, Sallust includes near the

beginning of his book on Catiline his own archaeology that offers his ideas on the rise and
fall of power.

Why Does a Republic Rise and Fall?

In contrast to Thucydides, Sallust did not think
it was wealth that made a state powerful. At
least, wealth was not the real basis for Rome's
power. Virtuous character was. After the Romans threw out the kings who ruled their city
in the early days and established republican government, citizens competed with one another
for glory. Each man wanted to be the first to
strike the enemy down, the first to climb the
walls in a siege, and this valor delivered amaz-
ing victories. Strength of character and mind
made Romans dominant. But a turning point
was reached with the destruction of Rome's
greatest rival, Carthage, in 146. Without the fear
of a foreign enemy, Romans suddenly found leisure and wealth more appealing. A longing for
money and power took hold of citizens—and
the moral inversion began. Greed taught arrogance and cruelty; ambition made men deceitful.
Sulla's march on Rome, the rampage he allowed

his army in the province of Asia, and the murders and plundering in Italy that accompanied his final victory were the natural result. And after Sulla's example, it only became worse. The powerful "few" felt more than ever that the state was theirs to dominate. In desperation, the ordinary citizens, oppressed with debt, were willing to embrace a dubious champion like Catiline.

In his later writings, Sallust would develop his idea that it was the fear of a foreign enemy that united the Romans, moderated their behavior, and made them act selflessly on behalf of the Republic.[12] Materially, the fall of Carthage made no real difference, but it did relax Romans' minds, blunt their courage, and make them succumb to natural desires for wealth, power, and pleasure. These effects unleashed the power struggles in Rome that turned into civil war—in Sulla's day, during the year of Catiline's conspiracy, and in the late 40s as Sallust was writing. Scathing as Sallust is, his work, like Thucydides's history, is infused with a tragic sense of the devastation caused by civil war. *The War against Catiline* ends with a somber scene of Romans turning over the corpses on a battlefield and

recognizing the faces of old friends and even relatives.

Sallust's explanation of history is based on psychology and the character of individuals. Power comes not from wealth but, in fact, the opposite: wealth gradually makes a state impotent. The power of a state, especially a democratic state, comes from the ability of its ordinary citizens and their leaders to control themselves. "Do not think it was by arms that our ancestors made the Republic great out of something small," Sallust has Cato say; instead, it was "hard work at home, a just exercise of power abroad, and a mind . . . not addicted to crime and pleasure."

Most historians writing today find such an approach too moralizing and prefer to emphasize larger, more impersonal, forces in explaining the problems of the late Roman Republic. According to one view, the wealth that flooded into Rome with imperial expansion did not so much corrupt citizens as unleash a debate on what to do with it.[13] At times the debate was contentious enough to lead to violence, especially because the Roman political system, with overlapping power in the popular assembly and

the Senate, was not well equipped to resolve the disputes.

Likewise, modern scholars writing about the Catilinarian conspiracy have suggested that Sallust's moralizing is reductive. While Sallust does acknowledge the debt crisis of 63 and the threat it posed to peasants and city-dwellers alike, the personality of Catiline is foregrounded so much that all of the unrest seems to originate with him. In reality, Catiline did not create the unrest but rather simply seized on it.

There has been much skepticism, in particular, of Sallust's account of a meeting of the conspirators that Catiline was said to have held in June 64—an account that itself contains a flashback to Catiline's earlier plot to kill the incoming consuls of 65.[14] This so-called First Catilinarian Conspiracy may largely be a later invention that grew out of allegations first made by Cicero when he ran against Catiline in the consular elections of 64.[15] Sallust himself elsewhere acknowledges how readily stories about Catiline were made up. Did Catiline really pass around bowls of human blood mixed with wine? Did he have sex with the young men who supported him? Proof was lacking. As for the

meeting in 64, Sallust may attribute plans to Catiline that only developed later. An ancient historian was in some ways like a historical novelist. The historian typically wrote the elaborate speeches he has his protagonists give, and Catiline's speech calling for war in June 64 is a prime example. It helped Sallust suggest that Catiline was long bent on making war on his country.

But whether we put forward purely structural explanations of history that exclude personalities or dismiss Sallust's work as empty moralizing and rhetoric, we go too far—and we certainly miss what makes Sallust worth reading. Does anyone really think that the character of politicians and citizens has no impact on public life? Certainly early Americans, steeped in classical authors like Sallust, thought character to be of the profoundest importance and paid a great deal of attention to it as they built a new republic.

Hoping to retire from politics in 1800, Alexander Hamilton felt forced to return when the House of Representatives had to break the tie between the presidential candidates Thomas Jefferson and Aaron Burr. As much as Hamilton

disliked his old enemy Jefferson, Burr was far more dangerous in Hamilton's view. Hamilton wrote of Burr:

> His private character is not defended by his most partial friends. He is bankrupt beyond redemption except by the plunder of his country. His public principles have no other spring or aim than his own aggrandizement. . . . If he can he will certainly disturb our institutions to secure himself *permanent power* and with it *wealth*. He is truly the Catiline of America.[16]

As the historian Joseph Ellis writes, "No one in the political leadership of the early American republic needed to be reminded who Catiline was."[17] In making his attacks on Burr, Hamilton reached for the Roman conspirator as the quintessential example of the leader who puts private interests ahead of public ones. He was not trying to parade his classical education but rather to suggest the danger he thought Burr represented to the fragile new country. Like Cicero, Hamilton believed that it was his duty to denounce and defeat a threat to the republic, whatever the

personal cost. Ultimately, Hamilton paid with his life when Burr, serving in the office of vice president, shot him on the plains of Weehawken, New Jersey, in 1804.

If America has had a distinctively "paranoid style" of politics, one reason may be that charges of conspiracy are naturally at home in a republic, especially a large one with competing interests and fierce partisanship. In a sense, a successful conspiracy is the inversion of a republic—the triumph of the private interests of a few over the public interest of the rest.[18] Of course, when we speak of conspiracy, we may be indulging an entertaining fantasy or trying to smear an enemy. We may be exaggerating, for rhetorical purposes, actions taken by those in power or those who seek it to serve their own advantage, but with no real intention of toppling the government. As Sallust shows us, however, conspiracies do exist; if not stopped in time, a conspiracy may not destroy a republic, but it can still lead to civil war. And when a genuine conspiracy does arise, we need leaders brave and clever enough to face up to it and defeat it, while also taking into account the long-term consequences of their actions.[19] A

study of the past, Sallust reminds us, is a good way to learn what it takes to stop a conspiracy.

A Brief Note on Roman Names and Ranks, Dates, and Political Institutions at the Time of the Catilinarian Conspiracy

NAMES AND RANKS

A male citizen of Rome in the late Republic typically had a twofold or threefold name—for example, Gaius Antonius, Marcus Tullius Cicero, Lucius Sergius Catilina. The second name was the family name, and the (optional) third name distinguished branches of the family. The first name marked a man as an individual and could, for instance, distinguish brothers from each other. On first introducing a character, Sallust typically gives the full name but after that may just use one or two parts of it (for example, "Marcus Tullius" for Cicero).

In this period, a female citizen typically had just one name, which was the feminine form of the family name. Thus, Cicero's daughter was called Tullia. Sometimes a woman had a twofold name, to mark the branch of her family,

for instance Aurelia Orestilla (Catiline's wife at the time of the conspiracy).

Like other Roman authors, Sallust, in introducing a new character, often includes a word or two to indicate the character's social status: "Lucius Vargunteius, a senator"; "Fulvia, a noble woman"; "Gaius Cornelius, an equestrian." Senators were those who held major political office. Equestrians had to meet a high property requirement; they did not serve in political office but had other public roles, such as serving on juries in criminal trials.

Patricians were members of a few dozen distinguished families who traced their ancestry back to the earliest days of Rome. Everyone else—even Romans whose families had held office for several centuries—were plebeians. The "nobles" (*nobiles*, in Latin, literally, "the well-known") were those descended from consuls through the male line; they could be patrician or plebeian.

DATES

The Roman year was generally referred to by the names of the two consuls holding office, for example, "the consulship of Lucius Caesar and

Gaius Figulus" = 64 BC. The dating system was more complicated. Dates were reckoned backwards from the first day of the month, the Kalends, as well as two later days, the Ides and the Nones. Sallust includes few dates, and I have converted them into modern equivalents.

POLITICAL INSTITUTIONS

Describing in full the structure of Roman government is beyond the scope of this introduction—and not essential for understanding Sallust's narrative. But a few explanations are in order.

Rome's major political officers, known as "magistrates" (*magistratus*), were elected annually by popular assemblies. They held office for a year and—to prevent a monopoly of power—always shared office with at least one colleague. The following lists the officers, from lowest to highest rank; the number of positions elected each year, in parentheses; and the officers' major function:

Quaestor (20): Ran the treasury in Rome
or handled other financial tasks
(including overseas)

Tribune of the plebs (10): Presided over
the plebeian assembly and proposed
legislation to it (patricians were
excluded from holding this office)
Aedile (4): Oversaw the grain supply,
festivals, and buildings of Rome
Praetors (8): Administered the legal
system in Rome
Consuls (2): Served as the heads of state

Additionally, two censors were elected every
five years to take the census and revise the Senate membership.

The Senate was made up of five hundred to
six hundred members who, in principle, held
membership for life after holding the position of
quaestor. Strictly speaking, the Senate's role was
to advise the magistrates by issuing decrees
voted on after debate. By tradition, it made decisions on finance and foreign policy. It always
met indoors, either in the custom-built Senate-house (the Curia) or a temple.

There were several popular assemblies in
Rome. Their main functions were to elect magistrates and to vote on laws presented to them by
the magistrates. Voting was conducted by secret

ballot. Much of the legislation in the late Republic was voted on by the plebeian assembly, presided over by tribunes of the plebs; patricians were excluded from these deliberations.

There was no debate at voting assemblies themselves, but magistrates could call public meetings—usually in the Forum—to discuss pending legislation, decisions made by the Senate, and other matters of public importance.

The official name of the state was "the Roman People."

THE WAR AGAINST CATILINE

1 Omnis homines qui sese student praestare ceteris animalibus summa ope niti decet ne vitam
silentio transeant veluti pecora, quae natura
prona atque ventri oboedientia finxit. 2 Sed
nostra omnis vis in animo et corpore sita est.
Animi imperio, corporis servitio magis utimur;
alterum nobis cum dis, alterum cum beluis com-
mune est.

3 Quo mihi rectius [esse] videtur ingeni quam
virium opibus gloriam quaerere, et, quoniam
vita ipsa qua fruimur brevis est, memoriam nostri quam maxume longam efficere. 4 Nam divitiarum et formae gloria fluxa atque fragilis est,
virtus clara aeternaque habetur.

5 Sed diu magnum inter mortalis certamen
fuit vine corporis an virtute animi res militaris
magis procederet. 6 Nam et prius quam incipias

Introduction: The Strength of Mind over Body [1–3.2]

All men eager to rise above other animals ought to strain with all their might not to pass through life silently like cattle, which nature has made downward-facing and subservient to the stomach. Our full force as human beings is dependent on the mind as well as the body. We use our mind to rule, our body, more properly, to serve; the one we share with the gods, the other with beasts.

To me, therefore, it seems fitter to seek glory through the power of the intellect rather than physical strength, and, since the very life which we enjoy is short, to make remembrance of ourselves last as long as possible. The fame that wealth and beauty brings is fleeting and flimsy; excellence, a glorious and everlasting possession.

For a long time, however, there was a great dispute among men whether military affairs succeed more through strength of body or

consulto et, ubi consulueris, mature facto opus est. 7 Ita utrumque per se indigens alterum alterius auxilio eget. 2 Igitur initio reges—nam in terris nomen imperi id primum fuit—divorsi, pars ingenium, alii corpus exercebant.

Etiam tum vita hominum sine cupiditate agitabatur; sua cuique satis placebant. 2 Postea vero quam in Asia Cyrus, in Graecia Lacedaemonii et Athenienses coepere urbis atque nationes subigere, lubidinem dominandi causam belli habere, maxumam gloriam in maxumo imperio putare, tum demum periculo atque negotiis compertum est in bello plurumum ingenium posse.

3 Quod si regum atque imperatorum animi virtus in pace ita ut in bello valeret, aequabilius atque constantius sese res humanae haberent, neque aliud alio ferri neque mutari ac misceri omnia cerneres. 4 Nam imperium facile eis artibus retinetur quibus initio partum est. 5 Verum

excellence of mind. This is because before you undertake something, deliberation is needed, and once you have deliberated, speedy action. Each is insufficient on its own; one needs the help of the other. And so, in the beginning, kings—that was the first name on earth for supreme power—took opposite views: some developed their mind, others their body.

At that time, men still lived their lives without greed. Each was pleased enough with his own possessions. But after Cyrus in Asia, the Spartans and Athenians in Greece, began to conquer cities and nations, to treat a desire for domination as grounds for war, and to think that the greatest glory lay in the greatest power, then was it discovered through danger and difficulties that, in war, the intellect is most powerful.

Now, if the mental vigor of kings and generals were as powerful in peace as in war, human affairs would be more stable and constant. You would not see things going now one way, now another, everything changing and confused. For power is easily retained by those same practices by which it was first acquired. But when, in place of hard work, inactivity has taken over, in

ubi pro labore desidia, pro continentia et aequitate lubido atque superbia invasere, fortuna
simul cum moribus inmutatur. 6 Ita imperium
semper ad optumum quemque a minus bono
transfertur.

7 Quae homines arant, navigant, aedificant,
virtuti omnia parent. 8 Sed multi mortales, de-
diti ventri atque somno, indocti incultique vitam
sicuti peregrinantes transiere. Quibus profecto
contra naturam corpus voluptati, anima oneri
fuit. Eorum ego vitam mortemque iuxta aestumo, quoniam de utraque siletur.

9 Verum enim vero is demum mihi vivere
atque frui anima videtur qui aliquo negotio intentus praeclari facinoris aut artis bonae famam
quaerit.

Sed in magna copia rerum aliud alii natura
iter ostendit. 3 Pulchrum est bene facere rei publicae, etiam bene dicere haud absurdum est; vel
pace vel bello clarum fieri licet; et qui fecere et
qui facta aliorum scripsere multi laudantur.

place of self-restraint and fairness, lust and pride, then men's fortunes are transformed along with their character. In this way, power always passes to the best man from one less good.

What men sow, sail, or build: all of these depend on excellence. But many men, slaves to the stomach and to sleep, have passed through life untaught and uncultivated, as though they were traveling through a strange land. For them, nature was reversed—the body was a source of pleasure, the mind a burden. I attach the same value to their lives as to their deaths, seeing that nothing is said about either.

In fact, only that man seems to me truly to live and enjoy life who, bent upon some undertaking or other, seeks fame for a distinguished deed or noble conduct.

In the vast field of human activity, however, nature points one path to one man, a different one to another. To act well for the Republic is a glorious thing, and even to speak well for it is certainly not without merit. In peace or in war, you can become famous. Both those who have performed deeds and those who have written about the deeds of others win praise in great numbers.

2 Ac mihi quidem, tametsi haudquaquam par gloria sequitur scriptorem et auctorem rerum, tamen in primis arduum videtur res gestas scribere; primum, quod facta dictis exaequanda sunt, dehinc, quia plerique quae delicta reprehenderis malevolentia et invidia dicta putant. Vbi de magna virtute atque gloria bonorum memores, quae sibi quisque facilia factu putat, aequo animo accipit, supra ea veluti ficta pro falsis ducit.

3 Sed ego adulescentulus initio, sicuti plerique, studio ad rem publicam latus sum, ibique mihi multa advorsa fuere. Nam pro pudore, pro abstinentia, pro virtute audacia, largitio, avaritia vigebant. 4 Quae tametsi animus aspernabatur, insolens malarum artium, tamen inter tanta vitia imbecilla aetas ambitione corrupta tenebatur. 5 Ac me, cum ab relicuorum malis moribus dissentirem, nihilo minus honoris cupido eadem qua ceteros fama atque invidia vexabat.

And yet it seems to me that, while by no means the same glory falls on the writer and the originator of the actions, writing history is especially arduous. First, because deeds must be matched with words. And second, because most people think that whatever faults you have criticized were mentioned out of ill will and jealousy. When you recount the great prowess and the glory of good men, everyone readily accepts what he thinks would be easy for him to do; anything beyond that, like made-up stories, he considers untrue.

Sallust's Decision to Give up Politics and Write History [3.3–4]

As a young man, I was at first, like most others, drawn by a personal interest into politics. I faced many obstacles there. In place of modesty, self-restraint, and merit, it was shamelessness, bribery, and greed that flourished. Although my mind, unaccustomed to wicked practices, rejected these, nevertheless, in the midst of such great vices, ambition seduced my feeble youth and held it captive. Though I distanced myself from the bad behavior of the rest, desire for

4 Igitur, ubi animus ex multis miseriis atque periculis requievit et mihi relicuam aetatem a re publica procul habendam decrevi, non fuit consilium socordia atque desidia bonum otium conterere, neque vero agrum colundo aut venando, servilibus officiis, intentum aetatem agere. 2 Sed a quo incepto studioque me ambitio mala detinuerat eodem regressus statui res gestas populi Romani carptim, ut quaeque memoria digna videbantur, perscribere; eo magis quod mihi a spe, metu, partibus rei publicae animus liber erat.

3 Igitur de Catilinae coniuratione quam verissume potero paucis absolvam; 4 nam id facinus in primis ego memorabile existumo sceleris atque periculi novitate.

5 De cuius hominis moribus pauca prius explananda sunt quam initium narrandi faciam.

office still harmed me with the same awful reputation and envy as the others.

And so, when, after many distresses and dangers, my soul regained its calm and I decided that the rest of my life should be spent far away from public life, my intention was not to waste my valuable leisure in sluggish inactivity, nor to spend my life absorbed in farming or hunting—servile pursuits. Instead, returning to the same undertaking and interest from which evil ambition had kept me, I resolved to write down in separate works the achievements of the Roman People, to the degree that each event seemed worthy of remembrance. There was all the more reason to do so because my mind was free of hope, fear, and political partisanship.

I will, then, describe, briefly and as truthfully as I can, the conspiracy of Catiline, an event I regard as especially memorable for the novelty of the crime and its danger.

But I must first explain a few things about the character of this man before I begin my narrative.

5 L. Catilina, nobili genere natus, fuit magna vi et animi et corporis, sed ingenio malo pravoque. 2 Huic ab adulescentia bella intestina, caedes, rapinae, discordia civilis grata fuere, ibique iuventutem suam exercuit. 3 Corpus patiens inediae, algoris, vigiliae supra quam cuiquam credibile est. 4 Animus audax, subdolus, varius, cuius rei lubet simulator ac dissimulator; alieni adpetens, sui profusus; ardens in cupiditatibus; satis eloquentiae, sapientiae parum. 5 Vastus animus inmoderata, incredibilia, nimis alta semper cupiebat.

6 Hunc post dominationem L. Sullae lubido maxuma invaserat rei publicae capiundae, neque id quibus modis adsequeretur, dum sibi regnum pararet, quicquam pensi habebat. 7 Agitabatur magis magisque in dies animus ferox inopia rei familiaris et conscientia scelerum, quae utraque

Catiline [5.1–8]

Lucius Catiline, born into a noble family, had great strength of both mind and body, but a character vicious and degenerate. From his youth, civil wars, murder, plundering, and internal strife were agreeable to him, and it was in these pursuits that he spent his early manhood. His body could endure fasting, cold, and sleeplessness beyond anyone's capacity to believe. His mind was shameless, cunning, versatile—able to pretend or dissemble anything at all. Eager to take other men's property, he was prodigal with his own, and he burned in his desires. Adequate in eloquence, he lacked wisdom. Always his insatiable mind craved the extravagant, the incredible, the unattainable.

After the despotism of Lucius Sulla, a very great longing to capture the Republic had taken possession of Catiline, nor did he have any scruples by what means he would achieve this, so long as he secured power for himself. Every day his ferocious soul was tormented more and more by lack of money and guilt over his crimes, both of which he had increased by those practices I

eis artibus auxerat quas supra memoravi. 8 Incitabant praeterea corrupti civitatis mores, quos pessuma ac divorsa inter se mala, luxuria atque avaritia, vexabant.

9 Res ipsa hortari videtur, quoniam de moribus civitatis tempus admonuit, supra repetere ac paucis instituta maiorum domi militiaeque, quomodo rem publicam habuerint quantamque reliquerint, ut paulatim inmutata ex pulcherruma <atque optuma> pessuma ac flagitiosissuma facta sit, disserere.

6 Vrbem Romam, sicuti ego accepi, condidere atque habuere initio Troiani qui Aenea duce profugi sedibus incertis vagabantur, cumque his Aborigines, genus hominum agreste, sine legibus, sine imperio, liberum atque solutum. 2 Hi postquam in una moenia convenere, dispari genere, dissimili lingua, alius alio more viventes, incredibile memoratu est, quam facile coaluerint. <Ita brevi multitudo divorsa atque vaga concordia civitas facta erat.>

mentioned above. Also urging him on were the citizenry's corrupt morals, which were being ravaged by two most harmful, though mutually opposite, vices: extravagance and greed.

The Reason for Rome's Growth? Liberty [5.9–9]

My subject itself—since the occasion has made us think about the citizenry's morals—seems to encourage me to reach back in time and briefly discuss the habits of our ancestors, at home and on campaign. How did they manage the Republic and leave it so powerful? And how, gradually altered, did it go from being the finest and best to the worst and most disgraceful?

The city of Rome, as I have come to understand it, was founded and first inhabited by the Trojans, who, with Aeneas as their leader, were wandering in exile, with no settled home—and along with them the indigenous Italians, a rustic people without laws and without government, free and unrestricted. After these men came together into one city, although of disparate stock, speaking different languages, and each living his own way, with remarkable ease they united. In a brief space of time, a large and

3 Sed postquam res eorum civibus, moribus, agris aucta satis prospera satisque pollens
videbatur, sicuti pleraque mortalium haben-
tur, invidia ex opulentia orta est. 4 Igitur reges
populique finitumi bello temptare, pauci ex
amicis auxilio esse; nam ceteri, metu perculsi, a
periculis aberant.

5 At Romani, domi militiaeque intenti, festinare, parare, alius alium hortari, hostibus ob-
viam ire, libertatem, patriam parentesque armis
tegere.

Post, ubi pericula virtute propulerant, sociis
atque amicis auxilia portabant magisque dandis
quam accipiundis beneficiis amicitias parabant.
6 Imperium legitumum, nomen imperi regium
habebant. Delecti, quibus corpus annis infirmum,
ingenium sapientia validum erat, rei publicae
consultabant; ei vel aetate vel curae similitudine
patres appellabantur.

diverse group of wanderers had, by getting along, become a citizen body.

But after their state had grown in citizens, organization, and territory and was beginning to seem fairly powerful and prosperous, as is usual in human affairs, envy was born from wealth. Neighboring kings and peoples attacked, and only a few friends were of help; the rest, panic-stricken, held back from the dangers.

But the Romans, at home and on campaign, had their eye on everything; they hastened about, made plans, encouraged one another, threw themselves against their enemies, and protected with arms their freedom, their fatherland, and their parents.

Later, when they had through bravery warded off danger, they began to render aid to friends and to allies; more by giving favors than receiving them, they began to secure friendships. They had a government bound by law, which went under the name of monarchy. A select few, whose bodies were feeble in years but whose minds were strong in understanding, looked after the public interest. These men were called, by virtue of either their age or the similarity of their attentiveness, "the Fathers."[1]

7 Post, ubi regium imperium, quod initio conservandae libertatis atque augendae rei publicae
fuerat, in superbiam dominationemque se con-
vortit, inmutato more annua imperia binosque
imperatores sibi fecere; eo modo minume posse
putabant per licentiam insolescere animum
humanum.

7 Sed ea tempestate coepere se quisque magis
extollere magisque ingenium in promptu habere.
2 Nam regibus boni quam mali suspectiores sunt
semperque eis aliena virtus formidulosa est.
3 Sed civitas incredibile memoratu est, adepta
libertate, quantum brevi creverit; tanta cupido
gloriae incesserat. 4 Iam primum iuventus,
simul ac belli patiens erat, in castris per laborem
usu militiam discebat magisque in decoris armis
et militaribus equis quam in scortis atque con-
viviis lubidinem habebant. 5 Igitur talibus
viris non labor insolitus, non locus ullus asper
aut arduus erat, non armatus hostis formidulo-
sus. Virtus omnia domuerat.

6 Sed gloriae maxumum certamen inter ipsos
erat; se quisque hostem ferire, murum ascendere,
conspici dum tale facinus faceret properabat;

Later, when the monarchal government, which had first been instituted to preserve freedom and enlarge the state, degenerated into arrogance and tyranny, there was a change in regime, and they created for themselves offices held for one year, with two officers at a time.[2] This, they thought, would make it least possible for the human mind to grow overbearing through lack of restraint.

At that time, each man began to distinguish himself more and to display his talent more. This is because kings suspect good men more than bad and always dread excellence in another man. But once the state was in possession of liberty, it is remarkable how much it grew in a short time; such a great desire for glory had arisen. In the first place, young men, as soon as they were of an age to endure war, through toil and practice in the camp learned soldiering. They took pleasure more in splendid weapons and warhorses than in prostitutes and parties. For men like this, no toil was unfamiliar, no place rough or steep, no enemy in arms a source of dread. Valor had mastered everything.

But the fiercest contest for glory was among themselves. Each man hastened himself to strike

eas divitias, eam bonam famam magnamque no-
bilitatem putabant. Laudis avidi, pecuniae liberales erant; gloriam ingentem, divitias honestas
volebant. 7 Memorare possum quibus in locis
maxumas hostium copias populus Romanus
parva manu fuderit, quas urbis natura munitas
pugnando ceperit, ni ea res longius nos ab incepto traheret.

8 Sed profecto fortuna in omni re dominatur;
ea res cunctas ex lubidine magis quam ex vero
celebrat obscuratque. 2 Atheniensium res gestae,
sicuti ego aestumo, satis amplae magnificaeque
fuere, verum aliquanto minores tamen quam
fama feruntur. 3 Sed quia provenere ibi scripto-
rum magna ingenia, per terrarum orbem Atheniensium facta pro maxumis celebrantur. 4 Ita
eorum qui fecere virtus tanta habetur quantum
eam verbis potuere extollere praeclara ingenia.
5 At populo Romano numquam ea copia fuit,
quia prudentissumus quisque maxume negotio-
sus erat; ingenium nemo sine corpore exercebat;

the enemy, to climb the wall, to be seen while he did such a deed. This they considered wealth, this a good reputation and great nobility. Avid for praise, they were generous with their money; they wanted glory on a grand scale, wealth that was honorably acquired. I could recount in what places the Roman People with a small band routed very large armies of the enemy, what cities fortified by nature they took by assault, except that this would take me too far from my subject.

In everything, however, Fortune truly holds sway. She makes famous or obscures all matters according to her own fancy rather than the truth. The achievements of the Athenians, in my estimation, were glorious and grand enough, yet somewhat less than legend celebrates. But since writers of great talent sprang up from there, the deeds of the Athenians are talked about throughout the world as if they were the greatest. In this way, the excellence of those who performed the deeds is considered only as great as the splendid talents have been able to praise it in their words. But for the Roman People there never was this resource, since the cleverest men were also the busiest. Nobody trained his mind

optumus quisque facere quam dicere, sua ab
aliis benefacta laudari quam ipse aliorum narrare
malebat.

9 Igitur domi militiaeque boni mores cole-
bantur; concordia maxuma, minuma avaritia
erat; ius bonumque apud eos non legibus magis
quam natura valebat. 2 Iurgia, discordias, si-
multates cum hostibus exercebant, cives cum
civibus de virtute certabant. In suppliciis deorum magnifici, domi parci, in amicos fideles
erant. 3 Duabus his artibus, audacia in bello, ubi
pax evenerat aequitate, seque remque publicam
curabant.

4 Quarum rerum ego maxuma documenta
haec habeo, quod in bello saepius vindicatum est in
eos qui contra imperium in hostem pugnaverant
quique tardius revocati proelio excesserant quam
qui signa relinquere aut pulsi loco cedere ausi
erant; 5 in pace vero quod beneficiis quam metu
imperium agitabant et, accepta iniuria, ignoscere
quam persequi malebant.

without his body. The best men all preferred to act rather than to speak, to have their good deeds praised by others rather than to recount those of others themselves.

And so at home and on campaign, good morals were cultivated. Harmony was at its greatest, greed at its least. Right and goodness were strong with them naturally rather than through laws. Quarrels, disagreements, and feuds they carried on with their enemies; citizens competed with citizens over valor. In worship of the gods they were extravagant, at home frugal, and to friends faithful. By two practices—boldness in war and, when peace ensued, fairness—they cared for both themselves and the Republic.

For this I have the strongest proof. In war, there was more often punishment of those who fought an enemy against orders and who withdrew from battle too slowly when ordered back, than of those who dared to desert the standards or, if routed, to abandon their assigned position. In peace, on the other hand, our ancestors wielded power more through favors than fear, and if wronged, they preferred forgiveness to revenge.

10 Sed ubi labore atque iustitia res publica crevit, reges magni bello domiti, nationes ferae et
populi ingentes vi subacti, Carthago, aemula imperi Romani, ab stirpe interiit, cuncta maria
terraeque patebant, saevire fortuna ac miscere
omnia coepit. 2 Qui labores, pericula, dubias
atque asperas res facile toleraverant, eis otium
divitiae, optanda alias, oneri miseriaeque fuere.
3 Igitur primo pecuniae, deinde imperi cupido
crevit; ea quasi materies omnium malorum
fuere. 4 Namque avaritia fidem, probitatem ce-
terasque artis bonas subvortit; pro his superbiam,
crudelitatem, deos neglegere, omnia venalia habere edocuit.

5 Ambitio multos mortalis falsos fieri subegit, aliud clausum in pectore, aliud in lingua
promptum habere, amicitias inimicitiasque non
ex re sed ex commodo aestumare, magisque

The Curse of Leisure [10–13]

But when the Republic grew strong through hard work and fairness, when mighty kings were subdued in war, when fierce tribes and powerful peoples were overcome by force, when Carthage—the rival of Roman power—was destroyed root and branch, when all the seas and lands were laid open, then Fortune began to rage and throw everything into confusion.[3] Men who had readily tolerated toils, dangers, and doubtful and even desperate situations found leisure and wealth—desirable otherwise—a burden and a misfortune. First a longing for money, then for power, grew. These were, so to speak, the building blocks of all our misfortunes. Greed undermined loyalty, honesty, and other good practices. In place of these, it taught arrogance and cruelty, to neglect the gods and treat everything as up for sale.

Ambition drove many men to become deceitful, to keep one thing concealed in the heart and have another ready on the tongue, to value friendly and unfriendly relations not according to their real worth but their usefulness, to have

voltum quam ingenium bonum habere. 6 Haec primo paulatim crescere, interdum vindicari; post, ubi contagio quasi pestilentia invasit, civitas inmutata, imperium ex iustissumo atque optumo crudele intolerandumque factum.

11 Sed primo magis ambitio quam avaritia animos hominum exercebat, quod tamen vitium propius virtutem erat. 2 Nam gloriam, honorem, imperium bonus et ignavos aeque sibi exoptant; sed ille vera via nititur, huic, quia bonae artes desunt, dolis atque fallaciis contendit. 3 Avaritia pecuniae studium habet, quam nemo sapiens concupivit; ea, quasi venenis malis inbuta, corpus animumque virilem effeminat; semper infinita, insatiabilis est, neque copia neque inopia minuitur.

4 Sed postquam L. Sulla, armis recepta re publica, bonis initiis malos eventus habuit, rapere omnes, trahere, domum alius, alius agros cupere, neque modum neque modestiam victores habere,

a good outward appearance rather than inner character. At first, these practices increased gradually and sometimes were punished. Later, when the infection had spread like a plague, the city was transformed. The most just and honorable of governments became cruel and intolerable.

But at first, more than avarice it was ambition that troubled men's souls—a vice, certainly, but one that was closer to virtue. For a good man and a worthless one alike long for glory, honor, and power for themselves. But while the good man strives along the honest path, the worthless one, lacking in honorable skills, competes by trickery and deception. Avarice entails a yearning for money, which no wise man covets. As if steeped in strong poison, avarice weakens a virile body and mind. It is always unending, unsatisfied, slaked neither by abundance nor by dearth.

After Lucius Sulla took back the Republic by arms and, despite good beginnings, ended up doing wicked things, everyone was plundering and robbing, with one man coveting a house, another land.[4] The victors showed neither moderation nor mildness and committed foul cruelties

27

foeda crudeliaque in civis facinora facere. 5 Huc accedebat quod L. Sulla exercitum quem in Asia ductaverat, quo sibi fidum faceret, contra morem maiorum luxuriose nimisque liberaliter habuerat. Loca amoena, voluptaria facile in otio ferocis militum animos molliverant. 6 Ibi primum insuevit exercitus populi Romani amare, potare, signa, tabulas pictas, vasa caelata mirari, ea privatim et publice rapere, delubra spoliare, sacra profanaque omnia polluere. 7 Igitur ei milites, postquam victoriam adepti sunt, nihil relicui victis fecere. 8 Quippe secundae res sapientium animos fatigant; ne illi corruptis moribus victoriae temperarent.

12 Postquam divitiae honori esse coepere et eas gloria, imperium, potentia sequebatur, hebescere virtus, paupertas probro haberi, innocentia pro malevolentia duci coepit. 2 Igitur ex divitiis iuventutem luxuria atque avaritia cum superbia invasere; rapere, consumere, sua parvi

against fellow citizens. Added to that, Sulla had, contrary to the practice of our ancestors, treated the army that he had led into Asia with extravagance and excessive generosity in order to render it loyal to him. The pleasant and luxurious quarters where they passed their leisure promptly softened the soldiers' fierce spirit. There for the first time an army of the Roman People became accustomed to whoring around and drinking, to admiring statues, paintings, and embossed cups, to stealing from private individuals and communities, to stripping temples, to desecrating everything sacred and profane. As a result, those soldiers, after they gained victory, left nothing to the defeated. Prosperity enervates even the minds of those who are wise; still less would those men with their immoral ways be able to control themselves in victory.

After wealth began to be a source of honor and was accompanied by glory, power, and influence, excellence began to grow blunt, poverty to be regarded as a disgrace, integrity considered nastiness. And so, as a result of wealth, a love of pleasure and of money, along with arrogance, seized hold of the young. They plundered, they laid waste; they cared little for their own and

pendere, aliena cupere, pudorem, pudicitiam, divina atque humana promiscua, nihil pensi neque moderati habere.

3 Operae pretium est, cum domos atque villas cognoveris in urbium modum exaedificatas, visere templa deorum quae nostri maiores, religiosissumi mortales, fecere. 4 Verum illi delubra deorum pietate, domos suas gloria decorabant; neque victis quicquam praeter iniuriae licentiam eripiebant. 5 At hi contra, ignavissumi homines, per summum scelus omnia ea sociis adimere quae fortissumi viri victores reliquerant, proinde quasi iniuriam facere, id demum esset imperio uti.

13 Nam quid ea memorem quae nisi eis qui videre nemini credibilia sunt, a privatis compluribus subvorsos montis, maria constrata esse? 2 Quibus mihi videntur ludibrio fuisse divitiae; quippe quas honeste habere licebat, abuti per turpitudinem properabant.

3 Sed lubido stupri ganeae ceterique cultus non minor incesserat: viri muliebria pati, mulieres pudicitiam in propatulo habere; vescendi

coveted others' possessions; they disregarded modesty, chastity, everything divine and human; they had no scruples nor restraint.

It is worth your while, when you have seen houses and villas built out to the size of cities, to go look at the temples of the gods that our ancestors, most devout men, built. Out of dutiful respect they adorned the shrines of the gods, out of a sense of pride their houses, and they took nothing from the defeated, aside from the freedom to do wrong. The worthless Romans of today, on the other hand, have with out-and-out criminality snatched from our allies everything that the most valiant men had in their moment of victory left—as if to exercise power meant nothing but to commit injustice!

Why should I recount things believable only to those who have seen them: mountains leveled, seas paved over by more than a few private citizens?[5] For them, it seems to me, wealth was something to play with; what they could have treated honorably, they rushed to misuse in disgrace.

An equally strong desire for illicit sex, gluttony, and other self-indulgence had arisen. Men submitted to the women's role in sex, women put

causa terra marique omnia exquirere; dormire prius quam somni cupido esset, non famem aut sitim neque frigus neque lassitudinem opperiri, sed ea omnia luxu antecapere.

4 Haec iuventutem, ubi familiares opes defecerant, ad facinora incendebant.

5 Animus inbutus malis artibus haud facile lubidinibus carebat; eo profusius omnibus modis quaestui atque sumptui deditus erat.

14 In tanta tamque corrupta civitate Catilina, id quod factu facillumum erat, omnium flagitiorum atque facinorum circum se tamquam stipatorum catervas habebat. 2 Nam quicumque inpudicus, adulter, ganeo, manu, ventre, pene bona patria laceraverat, quique alienum aes grande conflaverat quo flagitium aut facinus redimeret, 3 praeterea omnes undique parricidae, sacrilegi, convicti iudiciis aut pro factis iudicium timentes, ad hoc quos manus atque lingua periurio aut sanguine civili alebat, postremo omnes quos

out their chastity for sale. To please the palate they sought out everything on land and sea. They went to bed before they had any desire for sleep. They did not wait for hunger or thirst, cold or fatigue, but through their extravagance prevented these in advance.

All of this filled the young men with a burning wish for crime, once their family wealth ran out. Souls steeped in bad practices did not easily forgo desires and, because of this, were more recklessly given over to every form of getting and spending money.

Catiline's Associates [14–16]

In so large and corrupt a city, Catiline had no difficulty in surrounding himself with bands of shameless and criminal men as if they were a guard. Every adulterer, glutton, or rake who had destroyed his inheritance by gambling, gorging, or sex; everyone who had piled up debt to release himself from disgrace or crime; all murderers of every background, and temple-robbers, and those convicted in the courts or fearing prosecution for their actions; those who were sustained by their hand and tongue with perjury

flagitium, egestas, conscius animus exagitabat, ei Catilinae proxumi familiaresque erant. 4 Quod si quis etiam a culpa vacuus in amicitiam eius inciderat, cotidiano usu atque illecebris facile par similisque ceteris efficiebatur.

5 Sed maxume adulescentium familiaritates adpetebat; eorum animi molles etiam et fluxi dolis haud difficulter capiebantur. 6 Nam ut cuiusque studium ex aetate flagrabat, aliis scorta praebere, aliis canes atque equos mercari, postremo neque sumptui neque modestiae suae parcere dum illos obnoxios fidosque sibi faceret. 7 Scio fuisse nonnullos qui ita existumarent iuventutem quae domum Catilinae frequentabat parum honeste pudicitiam habuisse; sed ex aliis rebus magis quam quod cuiquam id compertum foret haec fama valebat.

15 Iam primum adulescens Catilina multa nefanda stupra fecerat, cum virgine nobili, cum sacerdote Vestae, alia huiusce modi contra ius

or the bloodshed of fellow citizens; finally, all whom disgrace, poverty, a guilty conscience disturbed: these were the associates and personal friends of Catiline. And even if somebody free of fault had fallen into friendship with Catiline, daily intercourse and enticements promptly made him just like the rest.

Most of all, Catiline would seek out friendships with young men; their minds, still soft and unsteady, were easily ensnared through his cunning. In keeping with whatever desire age stirred in each of them, Catiline procured prostitutes for some, bought dogs and horses for others. In brief, he spared neither expenditure nor his own sense of honor, so long as he made them bound and devoted to him. There were some, I know, who thought that the youth who crowded Catiline's house were engaged in indecent sexual activity, but this rumor gained headway for reasons other than anybody actually having proof of it.[6]

In his own youth, Catiline, to begin with, committed many unspeakable sex crimes—with a girl of noble birth, with a priestess of Vesta— not to mention other acts like this against human and divine law.[7] Eventually he was seized with

fasque. 2 Postremo captus amore Aureliae Orestillae, cuius praeter formam nihil umquam
bonus laudavit, quod ea nubere illi dubitabat, timens privignum adulta aetate, pro certo credi-
tur necato filio vacuam domum scelestis nuptiis
fecisse. 3 Quae quidem res mihi in primis videtur
causa fuisse facinus maturandi. 4 Namque animus inpurus, dis hominibusque infestus,
neque vigiliis neque quietibus sedari poterat; ita
conscientia mentem excitam vastabat. 5 Igitur
colos ei exsanguis, foedi oculi, citus modo, modo
tardus incessus; prorsus in facie vultuque vecor-
dia inerat.

16 Sed iuventutem quam, ut supra diximus,
inlexerat, multis modis mala facinora edocebat. 2
Ex illis testis signatoresque falsos commodare;
fidem, fortunas, pericula vilia habere, post, ubi
eorum famam atque pudorem adtriverat, maiora
alia imperabat. 3 Si causa peccandi in praesens
minus suppetebat, nihilo minus insontis sicuti
sontis circumvenire, iugulare; scilicet ne per

love for Aurelia Orestilla, in whom, aside from her beauty, no good man ever found anything to praise. Because she was hesitating over marrying him, from fear of a fully grown-up stepson, it is thought certain that Catiline killed his son to free up his house for this wicked marriage. This murder, I believe, was the main reason he hastened forward the conspiracy. For his vile mind, hostile to gods and men, could not be calmed whether he was awake or asleep, feelings of guilt so ravaged his tortured conscience. His color was pale, his eyes bloodshot, his step now quick, now slow. In short, madness was written on his face and his expression.

But the youth whom, as I said above, he had enticed he thoroughly instructed in evil crimes. He drew from their ranks false witnesses and forgers; he made them regard honor, property, and prosecutions for criminal charges as of little value; and later, when he had rubbed out their good name and sense of shame, he demanded other, greater crimes. If there was no immediate reason for wrongdoing at hand? He still would attack innocent men as if they were guilty and slit their throats; doubtless to prevent hand

otium torpescerent manus aut animus, gratuito potius malus atque crudelis erat.

4 His amicis sociisque confisus Catilina, simul quod aes alienum per omnis terras ingens erat, et quod plerique Sullani milites, largius suo usi, rapinarum et victoriae veteris memores, civile bellum exoptabant, opprimundae rei publicae consilium cepit. **5** In Italia nullus exercitus; Cn. Pompeius in extremis terris bellum gerebat; ipsi consulatum petenti magna spes; senatus nihil sane intentus; tutae tranquillaeque res omnes: sed ea prorsus opportuna Catilinae.

17 Igitur circiter Kalendas Iunias L. Caesare et C. Figulo consulibus primo singulos appellare, hortari alios, alios temptare; opes suas, inparatam rem publicam, magna praemia coniurationis docere. **2** Vbi satis explorata sunt quae voluit, in unum omnis convocat quibus maxuma necessitudo et plurumum audaciae inerat. **3** Eo convenere senatorii ordinis P. Lentulus Sura, P. Autronius,

or mind from growing sluggish through inactivity, he chose to be gratuitously evil and cruel.

Catiline was confident in these friends and allies. At the same time, because there was rampant debt throughout the world and because a great number of Sulla's soldiers had squandered their property and, remembering the pillaging and victory of the old days, were longing for civil war, Catiline formed a plan to overthrow the Republic.[8] In Italy there was no army; Gnaeus Pompey was waging war at the ends of the earth; in the consular elections Catiline's prospects were good; the Senate was entirely unfocused; everything was safe and still—the perfect opportunity for Catiline.

A Meeting of the Conspirators (June 64) [17]

And so, around the first of June, in the consulship of Lucius Caesar and Gaius Figulus [64], Catiline called on men, individually at first, urging on some, sounding out others. He showed them the resources at his disposal, the Republic's lack of readiness, the large rewards of conspiracy. Once he had sufficiently ascertained what he wanted, he then summoned to one place

L. Cassius Longinus, C. Cethegus, P. et Ser. Sullae Ser. filii, L. Vargunteius, Q. Annius, M. Porcius Laeca, L. Bestia, Q. Curius; 4 praeterea ex equestri ordine M. Fulvius Nobilior, L. Statilius, P. Gabinius Capito, C. Cornelius; ad hoc multi ex coloniis et municipiis, domi nobiles. 5 Erant praeterea complures paulo occultius consili huiusce participes nobiles, quos magis dominationis spes hortabatur quam inopia aut alia necessitudo. 6 Ceterum iuventus pleraque, sed maxume nobilium, Catilinae inceptis favebat. Quibus in otio vel magnifice vel molliter vivere copia erat, incerta pro certis, bellum quam pacem malebant.

7 Fuere item ea tempestate qui crederent M. Licinium Crassum non ignarum eius consili fuisse; quia Cn. Pompeius, invisus ipsi, magnum exercitum ductabat, cuiusvis opes voluisse contra illius potentiam crescere, simul confisum, si

all those who had the greatest needs and were the most reckless. There assembled, from the senatorial order, Publius Lentulus Sura, Publius Autronius, Lucius Cassius Longinus, Gaius Cethegus, Publius and Servius Sulla (the sons of Servius), Lucius Vargunteius, Quintus Annius, Marcus Porcius Laeca, Lucius Bestia, and Quintus Curius; from the equestrian order, Marcus Fulvius Nobilior, Lucius Statilius, Publius Gabinius Capito, and Gaius Cornelius; and many from the towns of Italy, men of high rank at home. There were, besides, a fair number of nobles who were participating a little less openly in this plot, motivated more by the hope of domination than by poverty or some other need. Many of the youth, furthermore, especially the sons of the nobility, were favorable to Catiline's plans. Able to live in ease with splendor or softness, they preferred uncertainty over certainty, war rather than peace.

There also were at that time those who believed that Marcus Licinius Crassus was not ignorant of the plot.[9] The thought was that, because Gnaeus Pompey—whom Crassus hated—was in command of a substantial army, Crassus wished for anyone with influence to rise up against Pompey's

coniuratio valuisset, facile apud illos principem se fore.

18 Sed antea item coniuravere pauci contra rem publicam, in quibus Catilina fuit; 2 de qua quam verissume potero dicam. L. Tullo et M'. Lepido consulibus, P. Autronius et P. Sulla, designati consules, legibus ambitus interrogati poenas dederant. 3 Post paulo Catilina, pecuniarum repetundarum reus, prohibitus erat consulatum petere, quod intra legitumos dies profiteri nequiverat.

4 Erat eodem tempore Cn. Piso, adulescens nobilis, summae audaciae, egens, factiosus, quem ad perturbandam rem publicam inopia atque mali mores stimulabant. 5 Cum hoc Catilina et Autronius, circiter Nonas Decembris consilio communicato, parabant in Capitolio

power; also, Crassus was confident that if the conspiracy succeeded, he would easily be the leading man among them.

Flashback: The First Catilinarian Conspiracy (December 66–February 65) [18–19]

But earlier a few men had similarly conspired against the Republic, among them Catiline, about which I will speak as accurately as I can.[10] In the consulship of Lucius Tullus and Manius Lepidus [66], the consuls-elect, Publius Autronius and Publius Sulla, had been charged under the laws of electoral malpractice and punished. Shortly afterwards, Catiline, who had been indicted for extortion, was prevented from standing for the consulship because he had been unable to declare his candidacy within the legally prescribed period.

There was, at that same time, a certain Gnaeus Piso, a young noble of extreme recklessness who was in need and dangerously partisan; poverty and poor character were spurring him on to disturb the Republic. Around the 5th of December, Catiline and Autronius let Piso in on their plan and made preparations to kill the consuls Lucius

Kalendis Ianuariis L. Cottam et L. Torquatum consules interficere, ipsi fascibus correptis Pisonem cum exercitu ad optinendas duas Hispanias mittere. 6 Ea re cognita, rursus in Nonas Februarias consilium caedis transtulerant. 7 Iam tum non consulibus modo, sed plerisque senatoribus perniciem machinabantur. 8 Quod ni Catilina maturasset pro curia signum sociis dare, eo die post conditam urbem Romam pessumum facinus patratum foret. Quia nondum frequentes armati convenerant, ea res consilium diremit.

19 Postea Piso in citeriorem Hispaniam quaestor pro praetore missus est, adnitente Crasso, quod eum infestum inimicum Cn. Pompeio cognoverat. 2 Neque tamen senatus provinciam invitus dederat, quippe foedum hominem a republica procul esse volebat; simul quia boni complures praesidium in eo putabant et iam tum potentia Pompei formidulosa erat.

3 Sed is Piso in provincia ab equitibus Hispanis quos in exercitu ductabat iter faciens occisus

Cotta and Lucius Torquatus on the 1st of January [65] on the Capitoline and then to seize the fasces themselves and send Piso with an army to hold the two Spanish provinces.[11] When the plot was discovered, they postponed the assassination plan to the 5th of February. This time they were scheming to destroy not only the consuls but many senators, and if Catiline had not given the signal to his allies prematurely in front of the Senate-house, on that day the worst crime since Rome's foundation would have been carried out. Because the armed men had not yet gathered in sufficient numbers, the plan fell apart.

Piso subsequently was sent as governor to Nearer Spain through the exertions of Crassus, since Crassus had come to see that Piso was a fierce enemy of Gnaeus Pompey.[12] And yet the Senate had not been unwilling to assign the province, because it wanted the offensive man far away from the Republic, and also because a large number of good men thought that in Piso lay their defense; already by that time Pompey's power was a source of dread.

This Piso, while marching in the province, was killed by some Spanish cavalry under his command. There are those who say that the

est. 4 Sunt qui ita dicant, imperia eius iniusta, superba, crudelia barbaros nequivisse pati; 5 alii autem equites illos, Cn. Pompei veteres fidosque clientis, voluntate eius Pisonem adgressos; numquam Hispanos praeterea tale facinus fecisse, sed imperia saeva multa antea perpessos. 6 Nos eam rem in medio relinquemus. De superiore coniuratione satis dictum.

20 Catilina, ubi eos quos paulo ante memoravi convenisse videt, tametsi cum singulis multa saepe egerat, tamen in rem fore credens univorsos appellare et cohortari, in abditam partem aedium secedit atque ibi omnibus arbitris procul amotis orationem huiusce modi habuit.

2 'Ni virtus fidesque vostra spectata mihi forent, nequiquam opportuna res cecidisset; spes magna, dominatio in manibus frustra fuissent,

barbarians could not endure his unjust, arrogant, and cruel orders. Others maintain that those cavalry, old and loyal clients of Gnaeus Pompey, attacked Piso with Pompey's consent. Never, they say, besides this one time had the Spaniards committed such a crime, but they had previously endured many savage orders. We will leave the matter unresolved. About the earlier conspiracy enough has been said.

The Meeting of June 64 BC Continues and Catiline Gives a Speech [20–21]

Catiline, when he saw that those men whom I mentioned a little earlier had assembled, although he had had long and frequent discussions with them individually, still thought it would be useful to address them as a group with encouraging words. He withdrew to a hidden part of the house and there, with all witnesses banished, gave a speech like this.[13]

"If your courage and loyalty had not been sufficiently proven to me, this favorable opportunity would have passed in vain; great hopes and the absolute power within our grasp would be of no use; and I would not be pursuing the

neque ego per ignaviam aut vana ingenia incerta pro certis captarem.

3 'Sed quia multis et magnis tempestatibus vos cognovi fortis fidosque mihi, eo animus ausus est maxumum atque pulcherrumum facinus incipere, simul quia vobis eadem quae mihi bona malaque esse intellexi. 4 Nam idem velle atque idem nolle, ea demum firma amicitia est.

5 'Sed ego quae mente agitavi omnes iam antea divorsi audistis. 6 Ceterum mihi in dies magis animus accenditur, cum considero quae condicio vitae futura sit, nisi nosmet ipsi vindicamus in libertatem. 7 Nam postquam res publica in paucorum potentium ius atque dicionem concessit, semper illis reges, tetrarchae vectigales esse, populi, nationes stipendia pendere; ceteri omnes, strenui, boni, nobiles atque ignobiles, volgus fuimus, sine gratia, sine auctoritate, eis obnoxii quibus, si res publica valeret, formidini essemus. 8 Itaque omnis gratia, potentia, honos,

uncertain instead of the certain if I had to rely on faintheartedness or lightweight talents.

"But because in many critical situations I have found you fearless and faithful to me, I am emboldened to embark on a most splendid and glorious enterprise—also, because I have come to realize that what is good and bad for me is the same for you. To have the same wishes, the same dislikes: this alone is true friendship.

"The plans I have devised all of you already heard before separately. But every day my feelings are more inflamed when I think about what terms we will live on if, by our own efforts, we do not deliver ourselves into freedom. Since the Republic passed under the jurisdiction and sway of a powerful few, it is to those men always that kings and petty rulers have rendered tribute, to those men that peoples and nations have paid taxes. But all the rest of us, however energetic, however good, noble and undistinguished alike, we have been a mob without influence, without authority, beholden to those for whom, if the Republic were in good health, we would be a source of fear. All influence, power, honor, and wealth are in their hands, or where they want it;

49

divitiae apud illos sunt aut ubi illi volunt; nobis reliquere pericula repulsas iudicia egestatem.

9 'Quae quo usque tandem patiemini, o fortissumi viri? Nonne emori per virtutem praestat quam vitam miseram atque inhonestam, ubi alienae superbiae ludibrio fueris, per dedecus amittere?

10 'Verum enim vero, pro deum atque hominum fidem, victoria in manu nobis est. Viget aetas, animus valet; contra illis annis atque divitiis omnia consenuerunt. Tantum modo incepto opus est, cetera res expediet.

11 'Etenim quis mortalium cui virile ingenium est tolerare potest illis divitias superare quas profundant in extruendo mari et montibus coaequandis, nobis rem familiarem etiam ad necessaria deesse? Illos binas aut amplius domos continuare, nobis larem familiarem nusquam ullum esse? 12 Cum tabulas, signa, toreumata emunt, nova diruunt, alia aedificant, postremo omnibus modis pecuniam trahunt, vexant,

for us they have left dangers, defeats, prosecutions, and poverty.

"For how long, I ask, will you endure these things, you men of great valor? Isn't it better to die with courage than to lose in disgrace a life of misery and shame, in which you are the butt for others' arrogance?

"But truly, by all that is sacred to gods and men, victory lies within our grasp. Our youth is vigorous, our spirit strong. For those men, on the other hand, everything has wasted away with age and wealth. All that's needed is to make a start; the course of events will see to everything else.

"What man is there worthy of the name who can stand for those people to have so much money they pour it out on building over the sea and leveling mountains, while for us family property fails to support even necessities? Who can stand for them to join together two houses or more, while for us there is no family home anywhere? They buy paintings, statues, and embossed cups; they tear down new houses and build others; they completely waste their money and eat away at it. Still, despite the greatest folly,

tamen summa lubidine divitias suas vincere nequeunt. 13 At nobis est domi inopia, foris aes alienum, mala res, spes multo asperior; denique
quid relicui habemus praeter miseram animam?

14 'Quin igitur expergiscimini? En illa, illa
quam saepe optastis libertas, praeterea divitiae,
decus, gloria in oculis sita sunt; fortuna omnia
ea victoribus praemia posuit. 15 Res, tempus, pericula, egestas, belli spolia magnifica magis
quam oratio mea vos hortantur. 16 Vel impera-
tore vel milite me utimini; neque animus neque
corpus a vobis aberit.

17 'Haec ipsa, ut spero, vobiscum una consul
agam, nisi forte me animus fallit et vos servire
magis quam imperare parati estis.'

21 Postquam accepere ea homines, quibus
mala abunde omnia erant sed neque res neque
spes bona ulla, tametsi illis quieta movere magna
merces videbatur, tamen postulavere plerique ut

they cannot exhaust their wealth. But for us there is scarcity at home, debt outside it—a terrible situation, with a future far worse. What, in short, do we have left, aside from the wretched air we breathe?

"So why not wake up? Look! That freedom, that freedom you have often longed for, and wealth, honor, and glory too, are here before your eyes. All these are the prizes Fortune has set out for the victors. More than my speech, it is our present situation and the opportunity we have, our perils and our poverty, and the splendid spoils of war that urge you on. Use me as a commander or a soldier; neither my spirit nor body shall fail you.

"This is what I hope I will carry out with you as your consul, unless of course I am mistaken and you are prepared to be slaves rather than to rule."

It was men overwhelmed with every kind of misfortune but who had no resources and no honorable hope on whom these words fell. Even though disturbing the present tranquility seemed to them a large reward, nevertheless many insisted that he lay out what the terms of war would be, what prizes they would aim at by

proponeret quae condicio belli foret, quae praemia armis peterent, quid ubique opis aut spei haberent. 2 Tum Catilina polliceri tabulas novas,
proscriptionem locupletium, magistratus, sacer-
dotia, rapinas, alia omnia quae bellum atque lubido victorum fert. 3 Praeterea esse in Hispania
citeriore Pisonem, in Mauretania cum exercitu
P. Sittium Nucerinum, consili sui participes; petere consulatum C. Antonium, quem sibi collegam fore speraret, hominem et familiarem et
omnibus necessitudinibus circumventum; cum
eo se consulem initium agendi facturum.

4 Ad hoc maledictis increpabat omnis bonos;
suorum unum quemque nominans laudare;
admonebat alium egestatis, alium cupiditatis
suae, compluris periculi aut ignominiae, multos
victoriae Sullanae, quibus ea praedae fuerat.
5 Postquam omnium animos alacris videt, cohortatus ut petitionem suam curae haberent,
conventum dimisit.

force of arms, and what support they had or prospects of it, and where. Catiline then promised a wiping out of debts, a proscription of the wealthy, political offices, priesthoods, plundering, and everything else that war and the victor's fancy brings. Besides, he said, in Nearer Spain there was Piso, in Mauretania—with an army— Publius Sittius from Nuceria, and both were participants in his plot; Gaius Antonius was a candidate for the consulship, and Catiline hoped they would be colleagues; the man was a close friend and facing difficulties of every sort; as consul with him, Catiline would start his operation.[14]

In addition, Catiline attacked all the good men with slanderous allegations. His own supporters he praised, calling on each by name. He reminded one man of his poverty, another of his love of money, several more of their danger or disgrace, and many of the victory of Sulla and the plunder it had brought them. Seeing that everyone was full of enthusiasm, he urged them to devote themselves to his candidacy, and he then dismissed the meeting.

22 Fuere ea tempestate qui dicerent Catilinam, oratione habita, cum ad iusiurandum popularis sceleris sui adigeret, humani corporis sanguinem vino permixtum in pateris circumtulisse; 2 inde cum post execrationem omnes degustavissent, sicuti in sollemnibus sacris fieri consuevit, aperuisse consilium suum [atque eo dictitare fecisse] quo inter se fidi magis forent, alius alii tanti facinoris conscii. 3 Nonnulli ficta et haec et multa praeterea existumabant ab eis qui Ciceronis invidiam quae postea orta est leniri credebant atrocitate sceleris eorum qui poenas dederant. 4 Nobis ea res pro magnitudine parum comperta est.

Catiline Is Alleged to Have Bound Conspirators by Blood Oath [22]

At that time there were those who said that, after giving his speech, Catiline, at the moment he was binding the accomplices in his crime with an oath, passed around the blood of a human body mixed with wine in bowls. And then, when everyone had had a taste after the imprecation—just as customarily happens in sacred rites—he revealed his plot so that they would be more faithful to one another, sharing among themselves knowledge of the great atrocity. Some thought that this, along with much else, had been invented by those who believed that the hatred for Cicero that later arose was softened by the heinousness of the crime of the men who had been punished. Considering its magnitude, I regard this charge as insufficiently proven.

23 Sed in ea coniuratione fuit Q. Curius, natus haud obscuro loco, flagitiis atque facinoribus coopertus, quem censores senatu probri gratia moverant. 2 Huic homini non minor vanitas inerat quam audacia; neque reticere quae audierat neque suamet ipse scelera occultare, prorsus neque dicere neque facere quicquam pensi habebat.

3 Erat ei cum Fulvia, muliere nobili, stupri vetus consuetudo; cui cum minus gratus esset, quia inopia minus largiri poterat, repente glorians maria montisque polliceri coepit et minari interdum ferro, ni sibi obnoxia foret; postremo ferocius agitare quam solitus erat.

4 At Fulvia, insolentiae Curi causa cognita, tale periculum rei publicae haud occultum habuit sed, sublato auctore, de Catilinae coniuratione quae quoque modo audierat compluribus narravit. 5 Ea res in primis studia hominum

Cicero Elected Consul for 63 BC [23–24.2]

One of the conspirators was Quintus Curius, a man of not undistinguished birth, but deep in disgraceful and criminal acts; he had been removed from the Senate by the censors because of his shameful conduct. The foolishness of this man was as great as his recklessness. He cared not a bit about keeping to himself what he heard or concealing his own crimes. Indeed, he did not care about anything he said or did.

With Fulvia, a noble woman, he had an illicit affair of long standing. After he grew less satisfying to her—since, owing to his lack of resources, he could not make lavish gifts—all at once he started boasting and promising her the seas and the mountains, and sometimes he threatened her with a blade if she resisted him. In short, he was more aggressive than usual.

But Fulvia, having discovered the reason for Curius's arrogance, did not keep quiet about such a danger to the Republic but, without naming her informant, told a number of people what she had heard about Catiline's conspiracy and how. It was this action especially that

accendit ad consulatum mandandum M. Tullio Ciceroni. 6 Namque antea pleraque nobilitas invidia aestuabat, et quasi pollui consulatum credebant, si eum quamvis egregius homo novos adeptus foret. Sed ubi periculum advenit, invidia atque superbia post fuere.

24 Igitur comitiis habitis, consules declarantur M. Tullius et C. Antonius; quod factum primo popularis coniurationis concusserat. 2 Neque tamen Catilinae furor minuebatur, sed in dies plura agitare, arma per Italiam locis opportunis parare, pecuniam sua aut amicorum fide sumptam mutuam Faesulas ad Manlium quendam portare, qui postea princeps fuit belli faciundi.

3 Ea tempestate plurumos cuiusque generis homines adscivisse sibi dicitur, mulieres etiam aliquot, quae primo ingentis sumptus stupro corporis toleraverant, post, ubi aetas tantummodo

kindled men's enthusiasm for entrusting the consulship to Marcus Tullius Cicero. Previously, most of the nobility seethed with envy and considered the consulship practically polluted if a new man, however extraordinary, gained it. Yet when danger came, envy and arrogance were put aside.

And so the elections were held, and Marcus Tullius and Gaius Antonius were declared consuls, a result that gave the participants in the conspiracy their first shock. Catiline's frenzy, however, did not diminish. Every day he set more in motion, he assembled caches of weapons in strategically located spots throughout Italy, and he sent money borrowed on his own or his friends' credit to a certain Manlius in Faesulae, who later on was the first to make war.[15]

New Supporters for Catiline Include Women
[24.3–25]

Catiline is said at this time to have brought many men of every sort to his side, and even some women. In their younger days, these women had supported their profuse spending by defiling their bodies; later, when age had restricted only

quaestui neque luxuriae modum fecerat, aes alienum grande conflaverant. 4 Per eas se Catilina credebat posse servitia urbana sollicitare, urbem incendere, viros earum vel adiungere sibi vel interficere.

25 Sed in eis erat Sempronia, quae multa saepe virilis audaciae facinora commiserat. 2 Haec mulier genere atque forma, praeterea viro, liberis satis fortunata fuit; litteris Graecis, [et] Latinis docta, psallere, [et] saltare elegantius quam necesse est probae, multa alia quae instrumenta luxuriae sunt.

3 Sed ei cariora semper omnia quam decus atque pudicitia fuit; pecuniae an famae minus parceret, haud facile discerneres; lubido sic accensa ut saepius peteret viros quam peteretur.

4 Sed ea saepe antehac fidem prodiderat, creditum abiuraverat, caedis conscia fuerat, luxuria atque inopia praeceps abierat. Verum ingenium eius haud absurdum; posse versus facere, iocum movere, sermone uti vel modesto vel molli vel procaci; prorsus multae facetiae multusque lepos inerat.

their earnings and not their luxury, they piled up huge debt. Through them, Catiline believed that he could stir up the slaves in Rome, set the city ablaze, and attach their husbands to his cause—or kill them.

Among them was Sempronia, who had committed many deeds of manly recklessness.[16] This woman was quite fortunate in birth and beauty, in her husband and children too. She was skilled in Latin and Greek literature, in singing and dancing more attractively than is necessary for an honorable woman, and in many other things that are aids to indulgence.

Nothing was ever more worthless to her than honor or chastity. It would be hard to decide whether she spared her money or her reputation less. So burning was her desire that she more often sought out men than they sought her.

Previously, she had often broken her word, disavowed loans, been an accomplice in murder, and plunged headlong in luxury and destitution. But she had considerable talent. She could compose verses, make jokes, and engage in conversation that was modest, tender, or racy. In short, she had wit and charm.

26 His rebus conparatis, Catilina nihilo minus in proxumum annum consulatum petebat, sperans, si designatus foret, facile se ex voluntate Antonio usurum. Neque interea quietus erat, sed omnibus modis insidias parabat Ciceroni.

2 Neque illi tamen ad cavendum dolus aut astutiae deerant. 3 Namque a principio consulatus sui multa pollicendo per Fulviam effecerat ut Q. Curius, de quo paulo ante memoravi, consilia Catilinae sibi proderet. 4 Ad hoc collegam suum Antonium pactione provinciae perpulerat ne contra rem publicam sentiret; circum se praesidia amicorum atque clientium occulte habebat.

5 Postquam dies comitiorum venit et Catilinae neque petitio neque insidiae quas consulibus in campo fecerat prospere cessere, constituit bellum facere et extrema omnia experiri, quoniam quae occulte temptaverat aspera foedaque evenerant.

Catiline vs. Cicero [26–30.2]

These preparations notwithstanding, Catiline was still seeking the consulship for the following year in the hope that, if elected, he would easily use Antonius as he pleased.[17] Nor, in the meantime, did he remain quiet. He was preparing treacherous attacks of every kind on Cicero.

But Cicero did not lack guile or tricks to avoid harm. From the start of his consulship, by making large promises through Fulvia, he got Quintus Curius, about whom I spoke above, to betray Catiline's plans to him. Furthermore, through an agreement about provincial assignments, he prevailed on his colleague Antonius to stay loyal to the Republic.[18] Around himself Cicero kept a guard of friends and clients, without arousing notice.

Election day came. When neither Catiline's bid for office nor the attack he had made against the consuls on the Field of Mars succeeded, he decided to go to war and resort to the most extreme measures, since what he had tried to do furtively had ended unfavorably and with disgrace.[19]

27 Igitur C. Manlium Faesulas atque in eam partem Etruriae, Septimium quendam Camertem in agrum Picenum, C. Iulium in Apuliam dimisit, praeterea alium alio, quem ubique opportunum sibi fore credebat.

2 Interea Romae multa simul moliri, consulibus insidias tendere, parare incendia, opportuna loca armatis hominibus obsidere; ipse cum telo esse, item alios iubere, hortari uti semper intenti paratique essent; dies noctisque festinare, vigilare, neque insomniis neque labore fatigari.

3 Postremo, ubi multa agitanti nihil procedit, rursus intempesta nocte coniurationis principes convocat per M. Porcium Laecam, **4** ibique, multa de ignavia eorum questus, docet se Manlium praemisisse ad eam multitudinem quam ad capiunda arma paraverat, item alios in alia loca opportuna qui initium belli facerent, seque ad

He therefore sent Gaius Manlius to Faesulae and the adjacent part of Etruria, a certain Septimius who came from the town of Camerinum to the territory of Picenum, Gaius Julius to Apulia, and others to other places, wherever he thought somebody could be of use to him.

Meanwhile at Rome, he was toiling over many schemes at once, laying traps for the consuls, readying fires, and occupying suitable spots with armed men. Catiline carried a weapon, he ordered the others to do the same, and he urged them to be in a constant state of readiness and focus. Day and night he rushed about, stayed up at all hours, and never grew tired from sleeplessness or hard work.

Finally, when despite his many efforts nothing succeeded, once again in the dead of night he had Marcus Porcius Laeca call together the leading members of the conspiracy. At the meeting Catiline complained at length about their lethargy. He then explained that he had sent Manlius ahead to that large number of men he had readied to take up arms, he had done the same with others in other suitable places so they could initiate war, and he longed to join his army—if only first he could get rid of Cicero.

exercitum proficisci cupere, si prius Ciceronem oppressisset; eum suis consiliis multum officere.

28 Igitur perterritis ac dubitantibus ceteris, C. Cornelius, eques Romanus, operam suam pollicitus et cum eo L. Vargunteius, senator, constituere ea nocte paulo post cum armatis hominibus sicuti salutatum introire ad Ciceronem ac de inproviso domi suae inparatum confodere. **2** Curius ubi intellegit quantum periculum consuli inpendeat, propere per Fulviam Ciceroni dolum qui parabatur enuntiat. **3** Ita illi ianua prohibiti tantum facinus frustra susceperant.

4 Interea Manlius in Etruria plebem sollicitare egestate simul ac dolore iniuriae novarum rerum cupidam, quod Sullae dominatione agros bonaque omnis amiserat, praeterea latrones cuiusque generis, quorum in ea regione magna copia erat, nonnullos ex Sullanis coloniis quibus lubido atque luxuria ex magnis rapinis nihil relicui fecerat.

29 Ea cum Ciceroni nuntiarentur, ancipiti malo permotus, quod neque urbem ab insidiis

"He is the one," Catiline said, "who really interferes with my plans."

Therefore, while the others were frightened and hesitating, Gaius Cornelius, an equestrian, promised his help. He, along with Lucius Vargunteius, a senator, agreed that a little later that night they would go with armed men to Cicero—as if to pay a call—and then without warning assassinate him at home unprepared. Curius, seeing how great a danger threatened the consul, immediately reported, through Fulvia, to Cicero the trap that was being laid. So the two men were turned away at the door; they had undertaken such a wicked deed in vain.

Meanwhile, in Etruria, Manlius was inciting the common people to revolt. They were longing for revolution because of their poverty and resentment at their unjust treatment; under the tyranny of Sulla, they had lost their farms and all of their other property. Manlius also incited every sort of brigand—they were numerous in this region—and some of the Sullan colonists, whose lust and luxury had left nothing of their great plunder remaining.

News of this was brought to Cicero. Alarmed by the twofold danger—he could no longer

privato consilio longius tueri poterat neque exercitus Manli quantus aut quo consilio foret satis
compertum habebat, rem ad senatum refert, iam
antea volgi rumoribus exagitatam.

2 Itaque, quod plerumque in atroci negotio
solet, senatus decrevit darent operam consules
ne quid res publica detrimenti caperet. 3 Ea potestas per senatum more Romano magistratui
maxuma permittitur: exercitum parare, bellum
gerere, coercere omnibus modis socios atque
civis, domi militiaeque imperium atque iudicium
summum habere; aliter sine populi iussu nullius
earum rerum consuli ius est.

30 Post paucos dies L. Saenius senator in senatu litteras recitavit quas Faesulis adlatas sibi
dicebat, in quibus scriptum erat C. Manlium
arma cepisse cum magna multitudine ante diem
VI Kalendas Novembris. 2 Simul, id quod in tali
re solet, alii portenta atque prodigia nuntiabant,
alii conventus fieri, arma portari, Capuae atque
in Apulia servile bellum moveri.

protect Rome from treachery through his own efforts, nor did he know for sure how large Manlius's army was or what it intended—he brought the matter, which had already been a source of rumors among the people, before the Senate.

Then, as is generally the practice when dealing with a grave emergency, the Senate decreed that the consuls should ensure that the Republic suffer no harm.[20] This power, the greatest that is entrusted to a magistrate by the Senate in Roman usage, allows him to raise an army, wage war, have total control over allies and citizens, and take command and ultimate jurisdiction at home and on campaign. In no other circumstances, except with a popular decree, does the consul have authority in these areas.

A few days later, Lucius Saenius, a senator, read out in the Senate a letter that he said had been sent to him from Faesulae. According to it, Gaius Manlius had taken up arms with a large number of men on October 27. At the same time, as typically happens in such a situation, some men were reporting portents and prodigies; according to others, meetings were taking place, arms were being transported, and a slave war was being stirred up at Capua and in Apulia.[21]

3 Igitur senati decreto Q. Marcius Rex Faesulas, Q. Metellus Creticus in Apuliam circumque ea loca missi—4 hi utrique ad urbem imperatores erant, inpediti ne triumpharent calumnia paucorum quibus omnia honesta atque inhonesta vendere mos erat—5 sed praetores Q. Pompeius Rufus Capuam, Q. Metellus Celer in agrum Picenum, eisque permissum uti pro tempore atque periculo exercitum conpararent. 6 Ad hoc, si quis indicavisset de coniuratione quae contra rem publicam facta erat, praemium servo libertatem et sestertia centum, libero inpunitatem eius rei et sestertia ducenta [milia]; 7 itemque decrevere uti gladiatoriae familiae Capuam et in cetera municipia distribuerentur pro cuiusque opibus, Romae per totam urbem vigiliae haberentur eisque minores magistratus praeessent.

Catiline Leaves Rome [30.3–32.1]

Therefore, by decree of the Senate, Quintus Marcius Rex was sent to Faesulae, and Quintus Metellus Creticus to Apulia and its environs. (Both of these men were on the outskirts of Rome, victorious commanders who had been blocked from celebrating a triumph by the petty quibbling of a few men who were in the habit of asking a price for everything, honorable and dishonorable alike.) The praetors Quintus Pompeius Rufus and Quintus Metellus Celer were sent to Capua and Picenum, respectively, and they were authorized to raise an army proportionate to the situation and the danger it posed. In addition, if anybody supplied information on the conspiracy that had been undertaken against the Republic, the reward for a slave was freedom and 100,000 sesterces, for a free man a pardon and 200,000 sesterces.[22] The senators also voted to distribute gladiatorial gangs to Capua and other towns, as the resources of each permitted, and in Rome to establish watches throughout the whole city, which were to be overseen by the lower-ranked magistrates.

31 Quibus rebus permota civitas atque inmutata urbis facies erat. Ex summa laetitia atque lascivia, quae diuturna quies pepererat, repente omnis tristitia invasit; **2** festinare, trepidare, neque loco neque homini cuiquam satis credere, neque bellum gerere neque pacem habere, suo quisque metu pericula metiri.

3 Ad hoc mulieres, quibus rei publicae magnitudine belli timor insolitus incesserat, adflictare sese, manus supplicis ad caelum tendere, miserari parvos liberos, rogitare omnia, <omni rumore> pavere, <adripere omnia> superbia atque deliciis omissis sibi patriaeque diffidere.

4 At Catilinae crudelis animus eadem illa movebat, tametsi praesidia parabantur et ipse lege Plautia interrogatus erat ab L. Paullo. **5** Postremo, dissimulandi causa aut sui expurgandi, sicut iurgio lacessitus foret, in senatum venit. **6** Tum M. Tullius consul, sive praesentiam eius

Citizens were alarmed by all of these developments, and the appearance of the city was transformed. After the great exuberance and wantonness that long-standing peace had given rise to, a sudden grim mood fell upon everyone. People rushed about and trembled in fear, no place or person was really trusted, there was not war but not peace either, and each person estimated the level of danger by his own anxiety.

Women, overcome by a terror of war they were not used to because of the Republic's great size, beat their breasts, stretched their hands to heaven in supplication, wept for their small children, kept asking about everything, at every rumor took fright, and seized on every bit of information. With pride and pleasures cast aside, they despaired for themselves and their country.

But the cruel mind of Catiline was turning over the same plans as before, even though defenses were being mounted and he himself had been arraigned by Lucius Paullus for violation of the Plautian Law.[23] Eventually, either to conceal his true purpose or to clear his name as if he had been slanderously attacked, he came into the Senate. Then Marcus Tullius the consul,

timens sive ira commotus, orationem habuit lu-
culentam atque utilem rei publicae, quam postea
scriptam edidit.

7 Sed ubi ille adsedit, Catilina, ut erat para-
tus ad dissimulanda omnia, demisso voltu, voce
supplici postulare a patribus coepit ne quid de
se temere crederent; ea familia ortum, ita se ab
adulescentia vitam instituisse ut omnia bona in spe
haberet; ne existumarent sibi, patricio homini,
cuius ipsius atque maiorum pluruma beneficia in
plebem Romanam essent, perdita re publica opus
esse, cum eam servaret M. Tullius, inquilinus
civis urbis Romae. 8 Ad hoc maledicta alia cum
adderet, obstrepere omnes, hostem atque parri-
cidam vocare. 9 Tum ille furibundus, 'quoniam
quidem circumventus' inquit, 'ab inimicis praeceps agor, incendium meum ruina restinguam.'

32 Deinde se ex curia domum proripuit. Ibi
multa ipse secum volvens, quod neque insidiae

either fearing Catiline's presence or stirred by anger, delivered a speech that was brilliant and beneficial to the Republic, and that he later distributed in writing.[24]

But when Cicero sat down, Catiline, ready as he was to hide everything, lowered his face and in a humble tone started to beg the senators to believe nothing about him without good reason. With the family he was born into and the life he had led from early manhood, he said, he could look forward to all good things. The senators should not think that he, a patrician who like his ancestors had done so many good deeds for the people of Rome, had any need to destroy the Republic when it was being protected by Marcus Tullius, a citizen of foreign birth![25] When he added other insults to this, everyone protested loudly and called him a public enemy and traitor. "Very well," he cried out, beside himself with rage, "since I am surrounded by enemies and brought to the brink, I will put out the fire I am threatened with by destruction."[26]

He then rushed out of the Senate to his home. There he went back and forth over many points in his mind. Because his plot against the consul was not making headway, and because he

consuli procedebant et ab incendio intellegebat urbem vigiliis munitam, optumum factu credens exercitum augere ac, prius quam legiones scriberentur, multa antecapere quae bello usui forent, nocte intempesta cum paucis in Manliana castra profectus est. 2 Sed Cethego atque Lentulo ceterisque quorum cognoverat promptam audaciam mandat, quibus rebus possent, opes factionis confirment, insidias consuli maturent, caedem, incendia aliaque belli facinora parent: sese propediem cum magno exercitu ad urbem accessurum.

3 Dum haec Romae geruntur, C. Manlius ex suo numero legatos ad Marcium Regem mittit cum mandatis huiusce modi.

33 'Deos hominesque testamur, imperator, nos arma neque contra patriam cepisse neque quo periculum aliis faceremus, sed uti corpora nostra ab iniuria tuta forent, qui miseri, egentes,

realized that the city was well protected against fire by the watches, he thought it best to increase his army and, before legions could be enrolled, to seize in advance many of the things that would be useful in war. In the dead of night, he set out with a few men for Manlius's camp. But he instructed Cethegus and Lentulus and the others whose bold recklessness he had come to recognize to strengthen the conspirators' resources however they could, to hurry forward the plot against the consul, and to plan murders, arson, and other crimes of war. As for himself, any day now, he said, he would march on the city with a great army.

A Plea to the Senate from the Indebted [32.3–34.1]

While this was taking place at Rome, Gaius Manlius sent envoys from his army to Marcius Rex with a message like this.[27]

"General, before gods and men alike we solemnly declare that we took up arms not against our fatherland, nor to endanger others, but to keep our bodies free from injury. Wretched and

violentia atque crudelitate faeneratorum plerique
patria sed<e>, omnes fama atque fortunis ex-
pertes sumus. Neque cuiquam nostrum licuit
more maiorum lege uti neque amisso patrimo-
nio liberum corpus habere; tanta saevitia faeneratorum atque praetoris fuit.

2 'Saepe maiores vostrum, miseriti plebis
Romanae, decretis suis inopiae eius opitulati
sunt; ac novissume memoria nostra propter
magnitudinem aeris alieni volentibus omnibus
bonis argentum aere solutum est. 3 Saepe ipsa
plebs, aut dominandi studio permota aut superbia magistratuum, armata a patribus secessit.

4 'At nos non imperium neque divitias peti-
mus, quarum rerum causa bella atque certa-
mina omnia inter mortalis sunt, sed libertatem,
quam nemo bonus nisi cum anima simul amit-
tit. 5 Te atque senatum obtestamur, consulatis
miseris civibus, legis praesidium quod iniqui-
tas praetoris eripuit restituatis, neve nobis

poverty-stricken, most of us have lost our family home through the violence and cruelty of the moneylenders, all of us our good name and our wealth. None of us has been allowed to enjoy the benefit of the law accorded by ancestral practice or, after the loss of property, to keep his body free, so great was the savagery of the money-lenders and the praetor.[28]

"Often your ancestors felt pity for the common people of Rome and through their decrees gave relief to the people's destitution. And very recently, within our own memories, debt had grown so large that it was written down to one-quarter of its value—with support from all the good men. Often the people themselves, roused by a desire to rule or by the contempt the magistrates felt for them, took up arms and seceded from the patricians.[29]

"But we, we do not seek power or wealth, the cause of all wars and struggles among men. We seek freedom, which no good man gives up except with his own life. We call on you and the Senate: consider the needs of citizens in misery, restore the protection of the law that the praetor unfairly snatched away, and do not force us

eam necessitudinem inponatis ut quaeramus quonam modo maxume ulti sanguinem nostrum pereamus.'

34 Ad haec Q. Marcius respondit, si quid ab senatu petere vellent, ab armis discedant, Romam supplices proficiscantur; ea mansuetudine atque misericordia senatum populi Romani semper fuisse ut nemo umquam ab eo frustra auxilium petiverit.

2 At Catilina ex itinere plerisque consularibus, praeterea optumo cuique litteras mittit: se falsis criminibus circumventum, quoniam factioni inimicorum resistere nequiverit, fortunae cedere, Massiliam in exilium proficisci, non quo sibi tanti sceleris conscius esset, sed uti res publica quieta foret neve ex sua contentione seditio oreretur.

3 Ab his longe divorsas litteras Q. Catulus in senatu recitavit, quas sibi nomine Catilinae redditas dicebat. Earum exemplum infra scriptum est.

to ask in what way we may perish so as best to avenge our bloodshed."

To this Quintus Marcius replied that, if they wished to ask the Senate for anything, they had to lay down arms and come to Rome in supplication. The Senate of the Roman People, he said, always was so mild and merciful that nobody ever requested its help in vain.

Catiline Pretends to Go into Exile [34.2–36.3]

As for Catiline, while en route he sent letters to most of the former consuls as well as all the best men. He had been unjustly convicted on false charges, he said. Since he could not effectively stand up against the clique of men hostile to him, he was yielding to fortune and setting off for Massilia in exile—not because he was guilty of a great crime, but so that the Republic would remain free from disturbance and no unrest would arise from a struggle undertaken by him.

Very different was the letter read out in the Senate by Quintus Catulus, which he said had been sent to him in Catiline's name.[30] Here is a copy of it.

35 'L. Catilina Q. Catulo. Egregia tua fides, re cognita, grata mihi magnis in meis periculis, fiduciam commendationi meae tribuit. 2 Quam ob rem defensionem in novo consilio non statui parare: satisfactionem ex nulla conscientia de culpa proponere decrevi, quam me dius fidius veram licet cognoscas.

3 'Iniuriis contumeliisque concitatus, quod fructu laboris industriaeque meae privatus statum dignitatis non obtinebam, publicam miserorum causam pro mea consuetudine suscepi; non quin aes alienum meis nominibus ex possessionibus solvere possem—et alienis nominibus liberalitas Orestillae suis filiaeque copiis persolveret—sed quod non dignos homines honore honestatos videbam meque falsa suspicione alienatum esse sentiebam. 4 Hoc nomine satis honestas pro meo casu spes relicuae dignitatis conservandae sum secutus.

5 'Plura cum scribere vellem, nuntiatum est vim mihi parari. 6 Nunc Orestillam commendo

"Lucius Catiline to Quintus Catulus. Your outstanding loyalty, known to me firsthand and so welcome in the midst of my great dangers, gives me confidence in entrusting affairs to you. I have, therefore, chosen not to make a formal defense of my new course of action, but I have decided to offer—not out of any feeling of guilt—an explanation which, so help me god, you may see is true.

"Angered by injuries and insults, deprived of the fruits of my hard work, and unable, as a result, to hold on to my position of prestige, I publicly took up, according to my habit, the cause of those in distress. It was not that I could not pay off debts undertaken in my own name using my possessions—and the generosity of Orestilla would have taken care of the debts in others' names using her and her daughter's wealth—but because I kept seeing unworthy men honored with office while I, I felt, had been treated as a public enemy on a false suspicion. It is on these grounds that I have followed the course of preserving what is left of my prestige—a course that is honorable enough, if you consider my plight.

"I wanted to write more, but news has come that force is being readied against me. And so I

tuaeque fidei trado; eam ab iniuria defendas, per liberos tuos rogatus. Haveto.'

36 Sed ipse paucos dies commoratus apud C. Flaminium in agro Arretino, dum vicinitatem antea sollicitatam armis exornat, cum fascibus atque aliis imperi insignibus in castra ad Manlium contendit. 2 Haec ubi Romae comperta sunt, senatus Catilinam et Manlium hostis iudicat, ceterae multitudini diem statuit ante quam sine fraude liceret ab armis discedere, praeter rerum capitalium condemnatis. 3 Praeterea decernit uti consules dilectum habeant, Antonius cum exercitu Catilinam persequi maturet, Cicero urbi praesidio sit.

4 Ea tempestate mihi imperium populi Romani multo maxume miserabile visum est. Cui cum ad occasum ab ortu solis omnia domita armis parerent, domi otium atque divitiae, quae prima mortales putant, affluerent, fuere tamen cives

entrust Orestilla to you for safekeeping; protect her from harm, as you love your own children, I beg you. Farewell."

Catiline stayed for a few days at the house of Gaius Flaminius in the territory of Arretium while he armed the populace, already in a state of unrest, and he then set out for the camp of Manlius with fasces and the other trappings of power. When this was learned at Rome, the Senate declared Catiline and Manlius public enemies; for the rest of the large force, a date was set by which they could disarm without penalty, except for those condemned for capital crimes. The Senate also decreed that the consuls should hold a military levy, Antonius and his army should hasten their pursuit of Catiline, and Cicero should protect Rome.

The People's Despair [36.4–39.5]

It was at this time, it seems to me, that the government of the Roman People was much the most miserable. The whole world, from the rising to the setting sun, had been tamed by arms and was submissive. At home, leisure and wealth—what men value most—were abundant.

qui seque remque publicam obstinatis animis perditum irent. 5 Namque duobus senati decretis ex tanta multitudine neque praemio inductus coniurationem patefecerat neque ex castris Catilinae quisquam omnium discesserat; tanta vis morbi ac ve<l>uti tabes plerosque civium animos invaserat.

37 Neque solum illis aliena mens erat qui conscii coniurationis fuerant, sed omnino cuncta plebes novarum rerum studio Catilinae incepta probabat. 2 Id adeo more suo videbatur facere. 3 Nam semper in civitate quibus opes nullae sunt bonis invident, malos extollunt; vetera odere, nova exoptant; odio suarum rerum mutari omnia student; turba atque seditionibus sine cura aluntur, quoniam egestas facile habetur sine damno.

4 Sed urbana plebes, ea vero praeceps erat de multis causis. 5 Primum omnium qui ubique probro atque petulantia maxume praestabant,

Yet there were still citizens who, with hardened hearts, were seeking to ruin themselves and the Republic. For despite the Senate's two decrees, no one out of such a large number of men had been induced by the rewards to reveal the conspiracy, and not a single person had defected from Catiline's camp. Such was the intensity of the disease that, like a plague, had attacked the souls of many citizens.

Nor was it only accomplices in the conspiracy whose minds were disturbed. The entirety of the common people were in favor of Catiline's undertakings because of their eagerness for revolution. This seemed exactly according to their habit; for in every state, those without wealth are prejudiced against the well-off and praise wicked men; they hate the old and long for the new; out of hatred of their situation, they desire for everything to change; they live off riot and sedition without anxiety, since for the poor it is hard to lose anything.

But the common people of the city of Rome especially were rash, for many reasons. First of all, those who most stood out anywhere for shameful conduct and insolence, then others

item alii per dedecora patrimoniis amissis, postremo omnes quos flagitium aut facinus domo expulerat, ei Romam sicut in sentinam confluxerant. 6 Deinde multi memores Sullanae victoriae, quod ex gregariis militibus alios senatores videbant, alios ita divites ut regio victu atque cultu aetatem agerent, sibi quisque, si in armis foret, ex victoria talia sperabat. 7 Praeterea iuventus, quae in agris manuum mercede inopiam toleraverat, privatis atque publicis largitionibus excita, urbanum otium ingrato labori praetulerat. 8 Eos atque alios omnis malum publicum alebat. Quo minus mirandum est homines egentis, malis moribus, maxuma spe, rei publicae iuxta ac sibi consuluisse.

9 Praeterea, quorum victoria Sullae parentes proscripti, bona erepta, ius libertatis inminutum erat, haud sane alio animo belli eventum expectabant. 10 Ad hoc quicumque aliarum atque senatus partium erant conturbari rem publicam quam minus valere ipsi malebant. 11 Id

who lost their property through their disgraceful ways, and then all those forced to leave home by crime or corruption had flowed into Rome as if into the bilge of a ship. Then there were many men who remembered Sulla's victory, and seeing some go from being simple soldiers to senators and others become so rich that they passed their whole lives in royal luxury, they each hoped, in taking up arms, for a similar outcome from their victory. There were young men, too, who by their own exertions had staved off poverty but, enticed by public doles and private bribes, preferred the ease of the city to thankless work. These and all the others were encouraged by the terrible state of public affairs. It is no wonder that men who were poverty-stricken, with loose morals and limitless ambitions, cared as little for the Republic as for themselves.

In addition, those whose parents had been proscribed when Sulla was victorious, their property seized and rights infringed on, looked forward to success in war with much the same attitude. Furthermore, those who belonged to a faction other than the Senate's preferred that the Republic be in turmoil rather than that they

<ad>eo malum multos post annos in civitatem revorterat.

38 Nam, postquam Cn. Pompeio et M. Crasso consulibus tribunicia potestas restituta est, homines adulescentes summam potestatem nacti, quibus aetas animusque ferox erat, coepere senatum criminando plebem exagitare, dein largiundo atque pollicitando magis incendere, ita ipsi clari potentesque fieri. 2 Contra eos summa ope nitebatur pleraque nobilitas senatus specie pro sua magnitudine. 3 Namque, uti paucis verum absolvam, post illa tempora quicumque rem publicam agitavere honestis nominibus, alii sicuti populi iura defenderent, pars quo senatus auctoritas maxuma foret, bonum publicum simulantes pro sua quisque potentia certabant. 4 Neque illis modestia neque modus contentionis erat; utrique victoriam crudeliter exercebant.

39 Sed postquam Cn. Pompeius ad bellum maritumum atque Mithridaticum missus est,

themselves not prevail. That very evil had, after many years, returned to the city.

This is because, following the restoration of the tribunes' power in the consulship of Gnaeus Pompey and Marcus Crassus [70], young men of impetuous age and temperament gained that great power. They began to stir up the common people by attacking the Senate, then to inflame them further with bribes and promises—all the while making themselves famous and power-ful.[31] Against them were most of the nobility, straining with all their might—ostensibly for the Senate's sake, but in reality to preserve their own great influence. To state the truth briefly, after that time, whoever disturbed the Republic on honorable pretexts—some claiming to defend the rights of the people, others to keep the in-fluence of the Senate supreme—though they were pretending to uphold the common good, were each fighting for their own power. Their struggle knew neither moderation nor mildness; both sides made cruel use of victory.

But once Gnaeus Pompey was sent out to wage war against the pirates and Mithridates, the influence of the common people waned

plebis opes inminutae, paucorum potentia crevit. 2 Ei magistratus, provincias aliaque omnia
tenere; ipsi innoxii, florentes, sine metu aetatem
agere, ceterosque iudiciis terrere, quo plebem in
magistratu placidius tractarent. 3 Sed ubi primum dubiis rebus novandi spes oblata est, vetus
certamen animos eorum adrexit. 4 Quod si
primo proelio Catilina superior aut aequa manu
discessisset, profecto magna clades atque calami-
tas rem publicam oppressisset neque illis qui
victoriam adepti forent diutius ea uti licuisset
quin defessis et exsanguibus qui plus posset imperium atque libertatem extorqueret.

5 Fuere tamen extra coniurationem complures
qui ad Catilinam initio profecti sunt. In eis erat
Fulvius, senatoris filius, quem retractum ex itinere parens necari iussit.

while the power of the few grew. These men held the magistracies, the provinces, and everything else. Unharmed, flourishing, they led lives free of fear while terrifying the others with the threat of prosecution so that those men would not rile up the common people while in office. Yet as soon as the situation became uncertain and hope of overthrowing the government presented itself, the old contest roused their passions. And if Catiline had come off the victor in the first battle or it had been a draw, there is no doubt that death and destruction would have overwhelmed the Republic. Those who had gained victory would not have been able to enjoy it for long but, pale and exhausted, would have had their power and freedom wrenched away by an individual of greater strength.[32]

Even so, there were many outside the conspiracy who went to join Catiline as it got under way. Among them was Fulvius, a senator's son, whose father ordered him dragged back from his journey and then killed.

6 Isdem temporibus Romae Lentulus, sicuti Catilina praeceperat, quoscumque moribus aut
fortuna novis rebus idoneos credebat, aut per se
aut per alios sollicitabat; neque solum civis, sed
cuiusque modi genus hominum, quod modo
bello usui foret.

40 Igitur P. Vmbreno cuidam negotium dat uti
legatos Allobrogum requirat eosque, si possit,
inpellat ad societatem belli, existumans publice
privatimque aere alieno oppressos, praeterea
quod natura gens Gallica bellicosa esset, facile
eos ad tale consilium adduci posse. 2 Vmbrenus,
quod in Gallia negotiatus erat, plerisque prin-
cipibus civitatium notus erat atque eos noverat.
Itaque sine mora, ubi primum legatos in foro
conspexit, percontatus pauca de statu civitatis et
quasi dolens eius casum requirere coepit quem
exitum tantis malis sperarent.

The Gauls Save Rome [39.6–45]

Meanwhile at Rome, just as Catiline had ordered, Lentulus either personally or through intermediaries strove to win over whomever he thought was suited to rebellion by character or circumstances—not only Roman citizens, but people of every sort, just so long as they were useful in war.

He then assigned a certain Publius Umbrenus to seek out the envoys of the Allobroges and push them into an alliance for war if he could. Lentulus's thought was that, because the Allobroges, both as a nation and individually, were crushed by debt, and because the Gallic people were naturally warlike to boot, they could easily be led into such an undertaking. Umbrenus, since he had done business in Gaul, was known to most of the leading members of the Gallic communities, and he knew them. And so, without delay, as soon as he saw the envoys in the Forum, he briefly inquired about the state of their country, and then, pretending to feel sorry for its misfortune, he began asking what end they hoped for to such great difficulties.

3 Postquam illos videt queri de avaritia magistratuum, accusare senatum quod in eo auxili
nihil esset, miseriis suis remedium mortem expectare, 'At ego' inquit, 'vobis, si modo viri esse
voltis, rationem ostendam qua tanta ista mala
effugiatis.'

4 Haec ubi dixit, Allobroges in maxumam
spem adducti Vmbrenum orare uti sui misere-
retur; nihil tam asperum neque tam difficile esse
quod non cupidissume facturi essent, dum ea res
civitatem aere alieno liberaret.

5 Ille eos in domum D. Bruti perducit, quod
foro propinqua erat neque aliena consili propter
Semproniam; nam tum Brutus <ab> Roma
aberat. 6 Praeterea Gabinium arcessit, quo maior
auctoritas sermoni inesset.

Eo praesente coniurationem aperit, nominat
socios, praeterea multos cuiusque generis
innoxios, quo legatis animus amplior esset.
Deinde eos pollicitos operam suam domum
dimittit.

41 Sed Allobroges diu in incerto habuere
quidnam consili caperent. 2 In altera parte erat

Umbrenus saw how they complained about the greed of the magistrates, how they attacked the Senate because it offered no aid, how they looked to death as the answer to their woes. He then said, "If only you want to be real men, I'll show you a way to escape all your great difficulties."

When he spoke these words, the Allobroges, filled with high hopes, begged Umbrenus to have pity on them. Nothing was so disagreeable or difficult, they said, that they would not do it eagerly, so long as it freed their people of debt.

Umbrenus brought them to the house of Decimus Brutus because it was near the Forum and not unfavorable for a meeting thanks to Sempronia. (Brutus was absent from Rome at the time.) Umbrenus also summoned Gabinius, to lend authority to what he said.[33]

In Gabinius's presence, Umbrenus revealed the plot, named the participants, and mentioned numerous other persons of every sort who were innocent, with a view to strengthening the envoys' spirits. After they promised their help, Umbrenus sent them home.

For a long time the Allobroges hesitated over what course to take. On the one hand was their

aes alienum, studium belli, magna merces in spe victoriae; at in altera maiores opes, tuta consilia, pro incerta spe certa praemia. 3 Haec illis volventibus, tandem vicit fortuna rei publicae. 4 Itaque Q. Fabio Sangae, cuius patrocinio civitas plurumum utebatur, rem omnem uti cognoverant aperiunt.

5 Cicero, per Sangam consilio cognito, legatis praecipit ut studium coniurationis vehementer simulent, ceteros adeant, bene polliceantur dentque operam uti eos quam maxume manufestos habeant.

42 Isdem fere temporibus in Gallia citeriore atque ulteriore, item in agro Piceno, Bruttio, Apulia motus erat. 2 Namque illi quos ante Catilina dimiserat inconsulte ac veluti per dementiam cuncta simul agebant: nocturnis consiliis, armorum atque telorum portationibus, festinando, agitando omnia, plus timoris quam periculi effecerant. 3 Ex eo numero compluris Q. Metellus Celer praetor, ex senatus consulto

debt, their passion for war, and a large reward hoped for in victory; on the other hand were superior resources, careful plans, and definite rewards instead of indefinite hope. As they were turning these points over in their minds, the fortune of the Republic in the end prevailed. And so they revealed the whole affair as they had learned of it to Quintus Fabius Sanga, on whose patronage their state most relied.

On learning of the plan through Sanga, Cicero instructed the envoys to feign strong support for the conspiracy, to approach the other conspirators, to make fair promises—and to take pains to get the clearest proof of their guilt.

Around the same time there was upheaval in Nearer and Further Gaul, and also in Picenum, Bruttium, and Apulia. Those men whom Catiline had earlier sent out were doing everything at once, incautiously, almost as if they were insane. With their nighttime meetings, their shipments of arms and weapons, their frenzied hurrying and disturbance of everything, they created more alarm than genuine danger. The praetor Quintus Metellus Celer, after holding a formal hearing in accordance with the Senate decree, threw many of them into irons. In

causa cognita, in vincula coniecerat, item in citeriore Gallia C. Murena, qui ei provinciae legatus praeerat.

43 At Romae Lentulus cum ceteris qui princeps coniurationis erant, paratis, ut videbatur, magnis copiis, constituerant uti, cum Catilina in agrum †faesulanum† cum exercitu venisset, L. Bestia tribunus plebis contione habita quereretur de actionibus Ciceronis bellique gravissumi invidiam optumo consuli inponeret; eo signo proxuma nocte cetera multitudo coniurationis suum quisque negotium exsequeretur.

2 Sed ea divisa hoc modo dicebantur: Statilius et Gabinius uti cum magna manu duodecim simul opportuna loca urbis incenderent, quo tumultu facilior aditus ad consulem ceterosque quibus insidiae parabantur fieret; Cethegus Ciceronis ianuam obsideret eumque vi adgrederetur; alius autem alium, sed filii familiarum,

Nearer Gaul, Gaius Murena, the officer in charge of that province, did the same.

But in Rome, Lentulus and the other leaders of the conspiracy, having gotten together what seemed to them a large force, decided that once Catiline had made it with his army to the territory of Faesulae, the tribune of the plebs Lucius Bestia would then convene a public assembly and denounce the actions of Cicero, pinning hatred for a very difficult war on the most excellent consul.[34] This would be the signal for the rest of the large number of conspirators to carry out on the following night the roles assigned to each of them.

The roles are said to have been divided like this. Statilius and Gabinius, along with a large gang of men, were to set fire simultaneously to twelve parts of the city, well chosen so that in the ensuing chaos it would be easier to get to the consul and the others against whom an attack was being mounted. Cethegus was to besiege the entry to Cicero's house and assault him violently. Other conspirators were assigned other victims, but the sons of certain families, especially those of the nobility, were to kill their

quorum ex nobilitate maxuma pars erat, paren-
tis interficerent; simul, caede et incendio percul-
sis omnibus, ad Catilinam erumperent.

3 Inter haec parata atque decreta Cethegus
semper querebatur de ignavia sociorum: illos
dubitando et dies prolatando magnas oppor-
tunitates corrumpere; facto, non consulto in
tali periculo opus esse, seque, si pauci adiuva-
rent, languentibus aliis impetum in curiam
facturum. 4 Natura ferox, vehemens, manu
promptus erat; maxumum bonum in celeri-
tate putabat.

44 Sed Allobroges ex praecepto Ciceronis per
Gabinium ceteros conveniunt. Ab Lentulo,
Cethego, Statilio, item Cassio postulant ius iu-
randum quod signatum ad civis perferant: aliter
haud facile eos ad tantum negotium inpelli
posse. 2 Ceteri nihil suspicantes dant; Cassius
semet eo brevi venturum pollicetur ac paulo ante
legatos ex urbe proficiscitur.

fathers. Then, with the city stunned by simultaneous murders and arson, they were to rush out to Catiline.

As these preparations and plans were being made, Cethegus complained constantly about the lethargy of his associates; by hesitating and putting off arrangements made for a particular day, they were losing great opportunities. "Action," he said, "not deliberation, is needed at such a critical moment. If a few of you will support me, even if the rest are weak and feeble, I'll attack the Senate-house!" Naturally aggressive, violent, quick to act, he thought the greatest advantage lay in speed.

The Allobroges, following Cicero's instructions, met with the other conspirators through Gabinius. From Lentulus, Cethegus, and Statilius, as well as Cassius, they demanded an oath that they might take, signed and sealed, to their countrymen; without it, their countrymen could not be easily led to join such an enterprise. The others suspected nothing and gave the oath; Cassius promised that he would come there soon, and he set out from Rome shortly before the envoys.

3 Lentulus cum eis T. Volturcium quendam Crotoniensem mittit ut Allobroges, prius quam domum pergerent, cum Catilina data atque accepta fide societatem confirmarent. 4 Ipse Volturcio litteras ad Catilinam dat, quarum exemplum infra scriptum est.

5 'Qui sim ex eo quem ad te misi cognosces. Fac cogites in quanta calamitate sis, et memineris te virum esse. Consideres quid tuae rationes postulent. Auxilium petas ab omnibus, etiam ab infumis.'

6 Ad hoc mandata verbis dat: cum ab senatu hostis iudicatus sit, quo consilio servitia repudiet? In urbe parata esse quae iusserit; ne cunctetur ipse propius accedere.

45 His rebus ita actis, constituta nocte qua profiscerentur, Cicero, per legatos cuncta edoctus, L. Valerio Flacco et C. Pomptino praetoribus imperat ut in ponte Mulvio per insidias Allobrogum comitatus deprehendant. Rem omnem

Lentulus sent, along with the envoys, a certain Titus Volturcius of Croton so that before the Allobroges reached home they could ratify their alliance with Catiline by exchanging pledges of good faith. Lentulus gave to Volturcius a letter for Catiline, a copy of which is given here.

"How I am doing you will learn from the man I have sent to you. Make sure you understand the great danger you're in and remember that you are a man! Consider what your plans require. Seek help from everyone, even the lowest."

Lentulus also gave verbal instructions: since Catiline had been declared a public enemy by the Senate, for what reason should he refuse to use slaves? In Rome, everything he had ordered was ready; he should not hesitate to move closer.

With these preparations complete and the night of the Allobroges' departure set, Cicero, apprised of everything by the envoys, gave orders to the praetors Lucius Valerius Flaccus and Gaius Pomptinus to catch the Allobroges and their escorts with an ambush on the Mulvian Bridge.[35] He explained to the praetors the background for why they were being sent but

aperit cuius gratia mittebantur; cetera uti facto opus sit ita agant permittit.

2 Illi, homines militares, sine tumultu praesidiis conlocatis, sicuti praeceptum erat, occulte pontem obsidunt. 3 Postquam ad id loci legati cum Volturcio venerunt et simul utrimque clamor exortus est, Galli, cito cognito consilio, sine mora praetoribus se tradunt. 4 Volturcius primo cohortatus ceteros gladio se a multitudine defendit, deinde, ubi a legatis desertus est, multa prius de salute sua Pomptinum obtestatus, quod ei notus erat, postremo timidus ac vitae diffidens velut hostibus sese praetoribus dedit.

46 Quibus rebus confectis omnia propere per nuntios consuli declarantur. 2 At illum ingens cura atque laetitia simul occupavere. Nam laetabatur intellegens, coniuratione patefacta, civitatem periculis ereptam esse; porro autem anxius erat, dubitans in maxumo scelere tantis

left them to manage the rest as the situation required.

They, being military men, without any commotion stationed their guards and secretly blockaded the bridge, just as they had been ordered. After the envoys came to this spot with Volturcius and there was shouting at the same time on both riverbanks, the Gauls quickly grasped the objective and immediately turned themselves over to the praetors. Volturcius at first urged on the others and defended himself with his sword against the large number of men. Then, when he was abandoned by the envoys, he made many pleas for safety to Pomptinus, because Pomptinus was known to him. Finally, fearful and despairing of his life, he surrendered to the praetors as if to an enemy.

Revelations in the Senate [46–47]

After this was accomplished, messengers quickly reported everything to the consul. Great worry and happiness simultaneously took hold of him. He was happy, because he saw that with the conspiracy out in the open, the city had been freed from danger. But he also was uneasy, hesitating

civibus deprehensis quid facto opus esset; poe-
nam illorum sibi oneri, inpunitatem perdundae
rei publicae fore credebat. 3 Igitur, confirmato
animo, vocari ad sese iubet Lentulum, Cethegum,
Statilium, Gabinium itemque Caeparium Ter-
racinensem, qui in Apuliam ad concitanda
servitia proficisci parabat. 4 Ceteri sine mora
veniunt; Caeparius, paulo ante domo egressus,
cognito indicio ex urbe profugerat.

5 Consul Lentulum, quod praetor erat, ipse
manu tenens in senatum perducit; relicuos cum
custodibus in aedem Concordiae venire iubet.
6 Eo senatum advocat magnaque frequentia eius
ordinis Volturcium cum legatis introducit;
Flaccum praetorem scrinium cum litteris quas
a legatis acceperat eodem adferre iubet.

47 Volturcius interrogatus de itinere, de litteris, postremo quid aut qua de causa consili
habuisset, primo fingere alia, dissimulare de

over what ought to be done after such important citizens had been caught in the greatest crime. Their punishment would be a burden for him personally, he thought; not to punish them would be the ruin of the Republic.[36] And so he strengthened his resolve and ordered Lentulus, Cethegus, Statilius, and Gabinius to be summoned before him, as well as a man from Terracina named Caeparius, who had been getting ready to set out for Apulia to stir up the slaves. The others came without delay, but Caeparius had left his house a little earlier and, after learning that the plot was revealed, had fled from Rome.

The consul personally took Lentulus by the hand into the Senate, because Lentulus was a praetor. The others were ordered to come under guard to the Temple of Concord.[37] There, Cicero summoned the Senate, and when it had assembled in full he brought in Volturicus with the envoys. He ordered the praetor Flaccus to carry in the writing case with the letters that he had obtained from the envoys.

Volturcius was asked about the journey, about the letters, and finally what plan he had made and why. At first, he invented a different story

coniuratione; post, ubi fide publica dicere iussus est, omnia uti gesta erant aperit docetque se, paucis ante diebus a Gabinio et Caepario socium adscitum, nihil amplius scire quam legatos, tantummodo audire solitum ex Gabinio P. Autronium, Ser. Sullam, L. Vargunteium, multos praeterea in ea coniuratione esse.

2 Eadem Galli fatentur ac Lentulum dissimulantem coarguunt praeter litteras sermonibus quos ille habere solitus erat: ex libris Sibyllinis regnum Romae tribus Corneliis portendi; Cinnam atque Sullam antea, se tertium esse cui fatum foret urbis potiri; praeterea ab incenso Capitolio illum esse vigesumum annum, quem saepe ex prodigiis haruspices respondissent bello civili cruentum fore.

3 Igitur, perlectis litteris, cum prius omnes signa sua cognovissent, senatus decernit uti,

and dissembled the facts of the conspiracy. Later, when he was ordered to speak with a guarantee of immunity, he disclosed everything as it had happened. He stated that he had been admitted as an accomplice by Gabinius and Caeparius a few days before and he knew nothing more than the envoys. From Gabinius he was accustomed to hear only that Publius Autronius, Servius Sulla, Lucius Vargunteius, and many others besides were in the conspiracy.

The Gauls testified similarly, and though Lentulus dissembled, they proved his guilt. Beyond his letter, they referred to conversations he had been in the habit of holding. According to the Sibylline books, supreme power in Rome was foretold for three men with the name of Cornelius, said Lentulus; Cinna and Sulla were earlier, and he would be the third for whom it was fated to be master of the city. He also said this was the twentieth year from the burning of the Capitoline, a year that the soothsayers had often declared, in response to portents, would be bloody with civil war.[38]

And so, when the letters had been read through in their entirety, with all the conspirators first having acknowledged their seals, the

abdicato magistratu, Lentulus itemque ceteri in liberis custodiis habeantur. 4 Itaque Lentulus P. Lentulo Spintheri, qui tum aedilis erat, Cethegus Q. Cornificio, Statilius C. Caesari, Gabinius M. Crasso, Caeparius—nam is paulo ante ex fuga retractus erat—Cn. Terentio senatori traduntur.

48 Interea plebs, coniuratione patefacta, quae primo cupida rerum novarum nimis bello favebat, mutata mente, Catilinae consilia exsecrari, Ciceronem ad caelum tollere; veluti ex servitute erepta gaudium atque laetitiam agitabat. 2 Namque alia belli facinora praedae magis quam detrimento fore, incendium vero crudele, inmoderatum ac sibi maxume calamitosum putabat, quippe cui omnes copiae in usu cotidiano et cultu corporis erant.

Senate decreed that Lentulus should resign from his magistracy and that he along with the others should be kept under the watch of individual guardians. Lentulus was turned over to Publius Lentulus Spinther, who was then an aedile; Cethegus to Quintus Cornificius, Statilius to Gaius Caesar, Gabinius to Marcus Crassus, and Caeparius—who a little earlier had been brought back from flight—to the senator Gnaeus Terentius.[39]

The Attempt to Implicate Crassus and Caesar
[48–49]

Meanwhile, with the conspiracy brought to light, the common people, who at first in their longing for revolution favored the war too much, now changed their minds. They cursed Catiline's plots and praised Cicero to the heavens. They showed joy and gladness as if they had been rescued from slavery. War's other wicked deeds they regarded as a source of profit more than loss, but fire was cruel, unrestrained, and most disastrous to them, since the only possessions they had were for everyday use and clothing the body.

3 Post eum diem quidam L. Tarquinius ad senatum adductus erat, quem ad Catilinam proficiscentem ex itinere retractum aiebant. 4 Is cum se diceret indicaturum de coniuratione si fides publica data esset, iussus a consule quae sciret edicere, eadem fere quae Volturcius de paratis incendiis, de caede bonorum, de itinere hostium senatum docet; praeterea se missum a M. Crasso qui Catilinae nuntiaret ne eum Lentulus et Cethegus aliique ex coniuratione deprehensi terrerent, eoque magis properaret ad urbem accedere, quo et ceterorum animos reficeret et illi facilius e periculo eriperentur.

5 Sed ubi Tarquinius Crassum nominavit, hominem nobilem, maxumis divitiis, summa potentia, alii rem incredibilem rati, pars tametsi verum existumabant, tamen quia in tali tempore tanta vis hominis magis leniunda quam exagitanda videbatur, plerique Crasso ex negotiis privatis obnoxii, conclamant indicem falsum esse, deque ea re postulant uti referatur.

On the next day, a certain Lucius Tarquinius was taken to the Senate; he was said to have been brought back from his journey while on the way to join Catiline. When Tarquinius said that he would provide information about the conspiracy in exchange for a guarantee of immunity, he was ordered by the consul to state publicly what he knew. He told the Senate more or less the same things that Volturcius had said about the planned fires, the slaughter of the good men, and the enemy's march. He also said that he had been sent by Marcus Crassus to tell Catiline not to be alarmed by the arrest of Lentulus, Cethegus, and other members of the conspiracy and to hasten his arrival in Rome. That way he would restore the others' spirits and make it easier to rescue from danger those under arrest.

When Tarquinius named Crassus, a noble with the greatest wealth and the highest power, some found it incredible; others, although they thought it true, nevertheless felt that in a crisis like this a man of such great weight ought to be appeased rather than antagonized. Many, too, were under obligation to Crassus as a result of private business transactions. In one voice they cried out that the informer was

6 Itaque, consulente Cicerone, frequens senatus decernit Tarquini indicium falsum videri eumque in vinculis retinendum neque amplius potestatem faciundam, nisi de eo indicaret cuius consilio tantam rem esset mentitus.

7 Erant eo tempore qui existumarent indicium illud a P. Autronio machinatum quo facilius, appellato Crasso, per societatem periculi relicuos illius potentia tegeret; 8 alii Tarquinium a Cicerone inmissum aiebant ne Crassus, more suo suscepto malorum patrocinio, rem publicam conturbaret. 9 Ipsum Crassum ego postea praedicantem audivi tantam illam contumeliam sibi ab Cicerone inpositam.

49 Sed isdem temporibus Q. Catulus et C. Piso neque precibus neque gratia neque pretio Ciceronem inpellere potuere uti per Allobroges aut alium indicem C. Caesar falso nominaretur. 2 Nam uterque cum illo gravis inimicitias exercebant: Piso oppugnatus in iudicio pecuniarum

lying, and they demanded formal consultation on the matter.

And so, asked by Cicero, a full Senate voted that Tarquinius's testimony appeared to be false, he should be kept in irons, and he should not have the right to testify further except to name the person on whose suggestion he had invented such a lie.

There were at that time those who thought that the testimony had been trumped up by Publius Autronius so that, with Crassus accused and involved in the danger, the rest might more easily be shielded by Crassus's power. According to others, it was Cicero who had instigated Tarquinus, in order to prevent Crassus from taking up, in his usual fashion, the defense of wicked men and thereby disturbing the Republic. I myself later heard Crassus personally assert that this grave reproach had been cast on him by Cicero.

At this same time, Quintus Catulus and Gaius Piso, whether by entreaty, by favor, or by outright bribery, were unable to prevail upon Cicero to have the Allobroges or some other informer falsely accuse Gaius Caesar. Both of these men nursed bitter hostility to Caesar—Piso

repetundarum propter cuiusdam Transpadani supplicium iniustum, Catulus ex petitione pontificatus odio incensus quod extrema aetate, maxumis honoribus usus, ab adulescentulo Caesare victus discesserat.

3 Res autem opportuna videbatur quod is privatim egregia liberalitate, publice maxumis muneribus grandem pecuniam debebat. 4 Sed ubi consulem ad tantum facinus inpellere nequeunt, ipsi singillatim circumeundo atque ementiundo quae se ex Volturcio aut Allobrogibus audisse dicerent magnam illi invidiam conflaverant, usque eo ut nonnulli equites Romani, qui praesidi causa cum telis erant circum aedem Concordiae, seu periculi magnitudine seu animi mobilitate inpulsi, quo studium suum in rem publicam clarius esset, egredienti ex senatu Caesari gladio minitarentur.

because while on trial in the extortion court he had been attacked by Caesar for unjustly punishing a man from Traspadane Gaul, and Catulus because he burned with hatred after his bid for the office of chief priest: advanced in age, having enjoyed the highest honors, he was beaten by Caesar, a youth.[40]

The occasion, furthermore, seemed suitable because Caesar, by remarkable generosity in private and the most splendid shows in public, owed a great deal of money. But when Piso and Catulus could not sway the consul to such a deed, they themselves, by individually going around and spreading lies about what they said they had heard from Volturcius or the Allobroges, aroused great hatred against Caesar. It reached the point that some Roman equestrians, who stood guard under arms around the Temple of Concord, were driven either by the extent of the danger or by their own impressionability to threaten Caesar at sword point as he came out of the Senate so that their own loyalty to the Republic would be more clear.

50 Dum haec in senatu aguntur et dum legatis Allobrogum et T. Volturcio, conprobato eorum indicio, praemia decernuntur, liberti et pauci ex clientibus Lentuli divorsis itineribus opifices atque servitia in vicis ad eum eripiundum sollici-tabant; partim exquirebant duces multitudi-num, qui pretio rem publicam vexare soliti erant. 2 Cethegus autem per nuntios familiam atque libertos suos, lectos et exercitatos, orabat in audaciam, ut grege facto cum telis ad sese inrumperent.

3 Consul ubi ea parari cognovit, dispositis praesidiis ut res atque tempus monebat, convo-cato senatu refert quid de eis fieri placeat qui in custodiam traditi erant. Sed eos paulo ante fre-quens senatus iudicaverat contra rem publicam fecisse.

4 Tum D. Iunius Silanus, primus sententiam rogatus quod eo tempore consul designatus erat,

The Senate Meets to Decide the Prisoners' Fate [50]

As all this was being done in the Senate and re-wards were being decreed for the envoys of the Allobroges and for Titus Volturcius (after their testimony had been verified), Lentulus's freed-men and a few of his clients scattered in differ-ent directions, trying to stir up craftsmen and slaves in the city's neighborhoods to rescue him. Some also were seeking out the gang leaders who had grown accustomed to causing public distur-bances in exchange for a bribe. Cethegus, too, using messengers, was begging his slaves and freedmen, a carefully selected and trained group of men, to take bold action; they should band to-gether and force their way to him with arms.

The consul, informed of these preparations, stationed guards as the situation advised and then convened the Senate and laid before it the question of what to do about the men who had been handed over into custody.[41] (Shortly be-fore, the full Senate had declared that they had acted treasonously.)

Decimus Iunius Silanus was asked his opin-ion first, since he was consul-elect at that time.

de eis qui in custodiis tenebantur, et praeterea de L. Cassio, P. Furio, P. Vmbreno, Q. Annio, si deprehensi forent, supplicium sumundum decreverat; isque, postea permotus oratione C. Caesaris, pedibus in sententiam Ti. Neronis iturum se dixit, qui de ea re praesidiis additis referundum censuerat. 5 Sed Caesar, ubi ad eum ventum est, rogatus sententiam a consule huiusce modi verba locutus est.

51 'Omnis homines, patres conscripti, qui de rebus dubiis consultant, ab odio, amicitia, ira atque misericordia vacuos esse decet. 2 Haud facile animus verum providet ubi illa officiunt, neque quisquam omnium lubidini simul et usui paruit. 3 Vbi intenderis ingenium, valet; si lubido possidet, ea dominatur, animus nihil valet.

4 'Magna mihi copia est memorandi, patres conscripti, quae reges atque populi, ira aut misericordia inpulsi, male consuluerint; sed ea

He declared that punishment should be inflicted on those who were being held in custody and also on Lucius Cassius, Publius Furius, Publius Umbrenus, and Quintus Annius, if they were caught. (Later, moved by the speech of Gaius Caesar, he said that he would join the motion of Tiberius Nero, who proposed that guards be increased and then the Senate should debate the matter.) But Caesar, when it came to his turn and he was asked his opinion by the consul, spoke like this.

Caesar Recommends Caution [51]

"Senate Fathers, all men who deliberate on uncertain matters ought to be free from hatred, friendship, anger, and pity. The mind does not easily perceive the truth when those emotions get in the way, nor did anyone ever heed his own desire and his own interest at the same time. When you have exerted your intellect, it prevails; if desire takes hold, desire rules, and the mind does not prevail.

"There is ample opportunity for me, Senate Fathers, to recall the poor decisions that kings and peoples have made under the influence of

malo dicere quae maiores nostri contra lubidinem animi sui recte atque ordine fecere. 5 Bello
Macedonico, quod cum rege Perse gessimus,
Rhodiorum civitas magna atque magnifica, quae
populi Romani opibus creverat, infida atque advorsa nobis fuit. Sed postquam, bello confecto,
de Rhodiis consultum est, maiores nostri, ne
quis divitiarum magis quam iniuriae causa bellum inceptum diceret, inpunitos eos dimisere.
6 Item bellis Punicis omnibus, cum saepe Car-
thaginienses et in pace et per indutias multa
nefaria facinora fecissent, numquam ipsi per
occasionem talia fecere; magis quid se dignum
foret quam quid in illos iure fieri posset
quaerebant.

7 'Hoc item vobis providendum est, patres
conscripti, ne plus apud vos valeat P. Lentuli et
ceterorum scelus quam vostra dignitas, neu
magis irae vostrae quam famae consulatis.
8 Nam si digna poena pro factis eorum reperi-
tur, novom consilium adprobo; sin magnitudo

anger or pity. But I prefer to talk about what our ancestors did rightly and properly, contrary to their desire. In the Macedonian War, which we fought against King Perseus, the great and glorious state of Rhodes, which had prospered with the help of the Roman People, was disloyal and hostile to us.[42] But after the war was brought to an end and the fate of the Rhodians was deliberated over, our ancestors let them go without punishment; nobody was to say that war had been undertaken for profit rather than because of injury. Again, in all of the Punic Wars, when the Carthaginians often had committed many treacherous acts both in times of peace and during truces, our ancestors never paid them back in kind when the opportunity offered. They asked what was worthy of themselves rather than what could justly be done against the Carthaginians.

"You, likewise, Senate Fathers, should see to it that the crime of Publius Lentulus and the others not outweigh your own standing, that you not heed your anger more than your reputation. If a penalty is found worthy of their actions, I am in favor of a novel measure. But if the scale of their crime surpasses everyone's

sceleris omnium ingenia exsuperat, his utendum censeo quae legibus conparata sunt.

9 'Plerique eorum, qui ante me sententias dixerunt composite atque magnifice casum rei publicae miserati sunt. Quae belli saevitia esset, quae victis acciderent enumeravere: rapi virgines, pueros, divelli liberos a parentum complexu, matres familiarum pati quae victoribus conlubuissent, fana atque domos spoliari, caedem incendia fieri, postremo armis, cadaveribus, cruore atque luctu omnia compleri.

10 'Sed, per deos inmortalis, quo illa oratio pertinuit? An uti vos infestos coniurationi faceret? Scilicet quem res tanta et tam atrox non permovit, eum oratio accendet!

11 Non ita est, neque cuiquam mortalium iniuriae suae parvae videntur; multi eas gravius aequo habuere. 12 'Sed alia aliis licentia est, patres conscripti. Qui demissi in obscuro vitam habent, si quid iracundia deliquere, pauci sciunt; fama atque fortuna eorum pares sunt. Qui magno imperio praediti in excelso aetatem agunt, eorum

imaginations, then I move that we make use of the penalties prescribed by the laws.

"Most of those who gave their opinions before me have deplored, in fine and impressive language, the misfortune of the Republic. They spelled out the savagery of war, the fate of the vanquished: girls carried off and raped, boys raped, children snatched from the embrace of their parents, mothers suffering whatever the victors wanted, temples and houses robbed, murder, conflagrations. In short, a world filled with weapons, corpses, blood, and sorrow.

"By the immortal gods, what was the point of that talk? Was it to make you hostile to the conspiracy? Of course a man who was not alarmed by so great and dreadful a deed will be aroused by a speech.

"Hardly! There is no one in the world who views the wrongs done to him as small; many feel them more deeply than is right. But not all men have the same freedom to act as they please, Senate Fathers. If the humble, who lead their lives in obscurity, do something wrong in a fit of temper, few know of it; their fame and fortune are paired. But those who, endowed with great power, spend their whole life in a high

facta cuncti mortales novere. 13 Ita in maxuma fortuna minuma licentia est; neque studere neque odisse sed minume irasci decet. 14 Quae apud alios iracundia dicitur, ea in imperio superbia atque crudelitas appellatur.

15 'Equidem ego sic existumo, patres conscripti, omnis cruciatus minores quam facinora illorum esse. Sed plerique mortales postrema meminere, et, in hominibus inpiis sceleris eorum obliti, de poena disserunt, si ea paulo severior fuit.

16 'D. Silanum, virum fortem atque strenuum, certo scio quae dixerit studio rei publicae dixisse neque illum in tanta re gratiam aut inimicitias exercere; eos mores eamque modestiam viri cognovi. 17 Verum sententia eius mihi non crudelis—quid enim in talis homines crudele fieri potest?—sed aliena a re publica nostra videtur.

18 'Nam profecto aut metus aut iniuria te subegit, Silane, consulem designatum, genus poenae novom decernere. 19 De timore supervacuaneum est disserere, cum praesertim diligentia clarissumi viri consulis tanta praesidia sint in

station—they do nothing without everyone learning of it. Therefore, with the greatest fortune comes the least freedom, and favoritism, hatred, and anger most of all are out of place. What in others is called a temper in one who has power is called arrogance and savagery.

"Senate Fathers, I personally believe that all tortures fall short of those men's crimes. But most people remember only what came last and, in the case of wicked men, they forget those men's crime and argue about their punishment, if it was a little too severe.

"I am sure that what Decimus Silanus, a courageous and energetic man, said, he said out of devotion to the Republic, nor is he influenced in so great a matter by personal feelings of sympathy or hostility. This I know to be the character, the restraint of the man. But his opinion does seem to me, not cruel—what can be cruel against men like that?—but foreign to our Republic.

"Undoubtedly it was fear or the seriousness of the offense that drove you, Silanus, a consul-elect, to propose a novel measure. About fear it is unnecessary to argue, especially since, thanks to the diligence of our most illustrious consul,

armis. 20 De poena possum equidem dicere, id quod res habet, in luctu atque miseriis mortem aerumnarum requiem, non cruciatum esse; eam cuncta mortalium mala dissolvere; ultra neque curae neque gaudio locum esse.

21 'Sed, per deos inmortalis, quam ob rem in sententiam non addidisti uti prius verberibus in eos animadvorteretur? 22 An quia lex Porcia vetat? At aliae leges item condemnatis civibus non animam eripi, sed exilium permitti iubent. An quia gravius est verberari quam necari? 23 Quid autem acerbum aut nimis grave est in homines tanti facinoris convictos? 24 Sin quia levius est, qui convenit in minore negotio legem timere, cum eam in maiore neglegeris?

25 'At enim quis reprehendet quod in parricidas rei publicae decretum erit? Tempus, dies, fortuna, cuius lubido gentibus moderatur. 26 Illis merito accidet quicquid evenerit; ceterum vos, patres conscripti, quid in alios statuatis considerate. 27 Omnia mala exempla ex rebus bonis

such large garrisons are under arms. As for the punishment, I can only say what is relevant to the issue. In grief and afflictions death is a respite from our troubles, not a torment. Death dissolves all of men's misfortunes; beyond it there is no place for worry or for joy.

"By the immortal gods, why, Silanus, did you not add to your resolution that they first be flogged? Was it because the Porcian Law forbids it?[43] Yes, but other laws similarly order that life not be ripped away from condemned citizens but exile be permitted. Is it because flogging is more severe than being put to death? But what is harsh or too severe against men convicted of such a wicked deed? If, on the other hand, flogging is milder than being put to death, what consistency is there in being frightened of the law on a smaller point when you have failed to observe it on a bigger one?

"Ah, but you say, who will criticize a decree passed against traitors to the Republic? Changing circumstances will, and the passage of time, and Fortune, whose pleasure rules nations. Whatever comes to pass for these men will be deserved; but, Senate Fathers, consider what sentence you are passing on others. All bad

orta sunt. Sed ubi imperium ad ignaros eius aut minus bonos pervenit, novom illud exemplum ab dignis et idoneis ad indignos et non idoneos transfertur.

28 'Lacedaemonii devictis Atheniensibus triginta viros inposuere qui rem publicam eorum tractarent. 29 Ei primo coepere pessumum quemque et omnibus invisum indemnatum necare; ea populus laetari et merito dicere fieri. 30 Post, ubi paulatim licentia crevit, iuxta bonos et malos lubidinose interficere, ceteros metu terrere. 31 Ita civitas, servitute oppressa, stultae laetitiae gravis poenas dedit.

32 'Nostra memoria victor Sulla cum Damasippum et alios eius modi, qui malo rei publicae creverant, iugulari iussit, quis non factum eius laudabat? Homines scelestos et factiosos, qui seditionibus rem publicam exagitaverant, merito necatos aiebant. 33 Sed ea res magnae initium cladis fuit. Nam uti quisque domum aut villam,

precedents have arisen from good actions. When power comes into the hands of men who are not acquainted with it or are crooked, that new precedent is transferred from the guilty, who deserve such treatment, to the innocent, who do not.

"After the Athenians were defeated, the Spartans set over them thirty men to manage their state.[44] These men started out by executing, without trial, all the most criminal men, objects of universal hated. The people rejoiced in the executions, saying they were deserved. Later, the freedom of the Thirty to do as they pleased grew; capriciously they killed good and bad alike and terrorized the rest with fear. So the citizens were crushed by slavery and paid a steep price for their foolish rejoicing.

"In our own time, when the victor Sulla ordered the throats slit of Damasippus and others like him who had grown powerful to the Republic's detriment, who was not celebrating that deed?[45] Wicked and dangerously partisan men, who had disturbed the Republic with their violent discord, deserved to be killed, it was said. But this was the start of a great massacre. Whenever anybody coveted the house or villa, even

postremo vas aut vestimentum alicuius concu-
piverat, dabat operam ut is in proscriptorum numero esset. 34 Ita illi quibus Damasippi mors
laetitiae fuerat paulo post ipsi trahebantur, neque
prius finis iugulandi fuit quam Sulla omnis suos
divitiis explevit. 35 Atque ego haec non in M.
Tullio neque his temporibus vereor; sed in
magna civitate multa et varia ingenia sunt. 36
Potest alio tempore, alio consule, cui item exercitus in manu sit, falsum aliquid pro vero credi.
Vbi hoc exemplo per senatus decretum consul
gladium eduxerit, quis illi finem statuet aut quis
moderabitur?

37 'Maiores nostri, patres conscripti, neque
consili neque audaciae umquam eguere; neque
illis superbia obstabat quominus aliena instituta,
si modo proba erant, imitarentur. 38 Arma atque
tela militaria ab Samnitibus, insignia magistratuum ab Tuscis pleraque sumpserunt; postremo,
quod ubique apud socios aut hostis idoneum
videbatur, cum summo studio domi exseque-
bantur; imitari quam invidere bonis malebant.

the plate or clothing, of another, he saw to it that the man was placed on the list of the proscribed. Thus, those for whom a little bit earlier Damasippus's death was a source of joy were soon dragged off themselves, and the throat-slitting only stopped when Sulla had glutted all his men with riches. I do not fear this happening with Marcus Tullius or in the present circumstances, but in a large body of citizens there are many different types of people. It is possible that in another situation, under another consul, who also has an army ready for use, some false accusation might be thought true. When, relying on this precedent, a consul draws his sword on the authority of a Senate decree, who will put a stop to him? Who will restrain him?

"Our ancestors, Senate Fathers, never lacked shrewdness or boldness. Pride did not stop them from imitating foreign customs, provided they were good. Arms and armor they adopted from the Samnites, most of the magistrates' insignia from the Etruscans. In short, whatever seemed useful among allies or enemies they re-created at home with the utmost enthusiasm; they liked to imitate good customs rather than be envious of them.

39 'Sed eodem illo tempore, Graeciae morem imitati, verberibus animadvortebant in civis, de condemnatis summum supplicium sumebant. 40 Postquam res publica adolevit et multitudine civium factiones valuere, circumveniri innocentes, alia huiusce modi fieri coepere. Tum lex Porcia aliaeque leges paratae sunt, quibus legibus exilium damnatis permissum est. 41 Hanc ego causam, patres conscripti, quominus novom consilium capiamus in primis magnam puto. 42 Profecto virtus atque sapientia maior illis fuit, qui ex parvis opibus tantum imperium fecere, quam in nobis, qui ea bene parta vix retinemus.

43 'Placet igitur eos dimitti et augeri exercitum Catilinae? Minume. Sed ita censeo: publicandas eorum pecunias, ipsos in vinculis habendos per municipia quae maxume opibus valent, neu quis de eis postea ad senatum referat neve cum populo agat; qui aliter fecerit, senatum existumare eum contra rem publicam et salutem omnium facturum.'

"But in that same period, imitating Greek practice, they flogged citizens and inflicted the supreme punishment on those found guilty. After the Republic became greater and, owing to the large number of citizens, factions grew strong, innocent men were hunted down, and other things like this started to happen. Then the Porcian Law was enacted, and other laws, which allowed those found guilty to go into exile. I consider this in particular as the main reason, Senate Fathers, why we should not adopt a novel measure. Surely those men who, from limited resources, made such a vast empire had greater valor and wisdom than we, who barely keep intact what they honorably acquired.

"Do I, therefore, recommend that these men be let go and the army of Catiline be strengthened? Not at all. This is my proposal: their money should be confiscated, they themselves should be kept in irons in the towns that are especially strong in resources, and nobody should refer their case again to the Senate or take it up in the popular assembly. The Senate will judge that whoever acts otherwise has acted against the Republic and the welfare of all."

52 Postquam Caesar dicundi finem fecit, ceteri verbo alius alii varie adsentiebantur. At M. Porcius Cato rogatus sententiam huiusce modi orationem habuit.

2 'Longe alia mihi mens est, patres conscripti, cum res atque pericula nostra considero et cum sententias nonnullorum ipse mecum reputo. 3 Illi mihi disseruisse videntur de poena eorum qui patriae, parentibus, aris atque focis suis bellum paravere; res autem monet cavere ab illis magis quam quid in illos statuamus consultare. 4 Nam cetera maleficia tum persequare ubi facta sunt; hoc nisi provideris ne accidat, ubi evenit, frustra iudicia inplores. Capta urbe nihil fit relicui victis.

5 'Sed, per deos inmortalis, vos ego appello, qui semper domos, villas, signa, tabulas vostras pluris quam rem publicam fecistis; si ista, cuiuscumque modi sunt quae amplexamini, retinere,

Cato Urges the Death Penalty [52]

After Caesar stopped speaking, the others said a word in support of one or the other proposal. But Marcus Porcius Cato, when asked his opinion, gave a speech like this.[46]

"Very different are my views, Senate Fathers, when I consider the situation and the danger facing us and when I reflect on the opinions offered by some members. They seem to me to have discussed the punishment due to those who have planned war against their fatherland, their parents, their altars, and their own hearths. The situation, however, demands that we defend against them rather than deliberate over what to do to them. Other crimes you may prosecute after they have been committed. But if you do not take care to stop this one from happening, once it does take place you will appeal to the courts in vain. In a captured city, there is nothing left for the vanquished.

"By the immortal gods, I beseech you, you who always have treated your houses, your villas, your statues, and your paintings as more valuable than the Republic: if you want to keep those things you have cherished, no matter of

si voluptatibus vostris otium praebere voltis, expergiscimini aliquando et capessite rem publicam. 6 Non agitur de vectigalibus neque de sociorum iniuriis; libertas et anima nostra in dubio est.

7 'Saepenumero, patres conscripti, multa verba in hoc ordine feci; saepe de luxuria atque avaritia nostrorum civium questus sum, multosque mortalis ea causa advorsos habeo. 8 Qui mihi atque animo meo nullius umquam delicti gratiam fecissem, haud facile alterius lubidini malefacta condonabam. 9 Sed ea tametsi vos parvi pendebatis, tamen res publica firma erat; opulentia neglegentiam tolerabat.

10 'Nunc vero non id agitur, bonisne an malis moribus vivamus, neque quantum aut quam magnificum imperium populi Romani sit, sed haec, cuiuscumque modi videntur, nostra an nobiscum una hostium futura sint. 11 Hic mihi quisquam mansuetudinem et misericordiam nominat?

what kind, if you want to provide the peace to enjoy your pleasures, wake up before it is too late and exert yourself for the Republic. We're not discussing taxes or the injuries done to our allies. It is our freedom, our lives that are in doubt.

"Very often, Senate Fathers, I have spoken at great length before this body. Often I have complained about the luxury and greed of our citizens, and as a result I have many men as my enemies. As one who never overlooked any offense in myself, even in my own thoughts, I could not easily pardon another man for misdeeds arising from his licentiousness. But although you regarded what I said of little value, still the Republic was strong; its abundance allowed for carelessness.

"Now, however, we are not discussing whether we live with good or bad morals, nor how large and fine the empire of the Roman People is, but whether all that we have, whatever we think of it, will be ours or will fall together with ourselves into the hands of the enemy. In such a situation as this, somebody speaks to me about mildness and mercy?

'Iam pridem equidem nos vera vocabula rerum amisimus; quia bona aliena largiri liberalitas, malarum rerum audacia fortitudo vocatur, eo res publica in extremo sita est. 12 Sint sane, quoniam ita se mores habent, liberales ex sociorum fortunis; sint misericordes in furibus aerari; ne illi sanguinem nostrum largiantur et, dum paucis sceleratis parcunt, bonos omnis perditum eant.

13 'Bene et composite C. Caesar paulo ante in hoc ordine de vita et morte disseruit, credo, falsa existumans ea quae de inferis memorantur, divorso itinere malos a bonis loca taetra, inculta, foeda atque formidulosa habere. 14 Itaque censuit pecunias eorum publicandas, ipsos per municipia in custodiis habendos, videlicet timens ne, si Romae sint, aut a popularibus coniurationis aut a multitudine conducta per vim eripiantur; 15 quasi vero mali atque scelesti tantummodo in urbe et non per totam Italiam sint, aut

"For a long time now we've lost the true meaning of words. Being lavish with other people's property is called generosity, boldness in carrying out bad deeds, bravery: this is why the Republic lies on the verge of destruction. By all means, since this is the way things are done now, let these men help themselves to the wealth of our allies; let them be merciful to those who rob the treasury! But let them not be lavish with our blood and, while they spare a few criminals, destroy all decent men!

"A moment ago before this body, in clear and impressive language, Gaius Caesar talked about life and death, considering untrue, I believe, what has been related about the underworld—how the wicked take a different path from the good and inhabit places that are nasty, neglected, foul, and frightful. He therefore proposed that the conspirators' property be confiscated and they themselves be held in custody through the towns of Italy, evidently fearing that if they were at Rome, accomplices in the conspiracy or a hired mob would rescue them by force. As if wicked and criminal men are only in Rome and not through all of Italy! As if boldness is not

non ibi plus possit audacia ubi ad defendundum opes minores sunt.

16 'Quare vanum equidem hoc consilium est, si periculum ex illis metuit; si in tanto omnium metu solus non timet, eo magis refert me mihi atque vobis timere. 17 Quare, cum de P. Lentulo ceterisque statuetis, pro certo habetote vos simul de exercitu Catilinae et de omnibus coniuratis decernere. 18 Quanto vos attentius ea agetis, tanto illis animus infirmior erit; si paululum modo vos languere viderint, iam omnes feroces aderunt.

19 'Nolite existumare maiores nostros armis rem publicam ex parva magnam fecisse. 20 Si ita esset, multo pulcherrumam eam nos haberemus, quippe sociorum atque civium, praeterea armorum atque equorum maior copia nobis quam illis est. 21 Sed alia fuere quae illos magnos fecere, quae nobis nulla sunt: domi industria, foris iustum imperium, animus in consulundo liber, neque delicto neque lubidini obnoxius.

more powerful where the defense against it is weaker!

"If, therefore, Caesar fears dangers from these men, his proposal is useless. If, in the midst of universal terror, he is the only one not to be afraid, all the more should I be afraid for myself and for all of you. Therefore, when you pass judgment on Publius Lentulus and the others, be clear that you are also making a decision about the army of Catiline and all the conspirators. The more carefully you handle this situation, the weaker their resolve will be. Let them see you droop even slightly, and they will all be here at once, full of fury.

"Do not think that it was by arms that our ancestors made the Republic great out of something small. If that were true, we would have it in a much finer state now, since we have larger numbers than they did of allies and citizens, not to mention arms and horses. But there were other qualities that made those men great, qualities we do not have at all: hard work at home, a just exercise of power abroad, and a mind free in deliberation, not addicted to crime and pleasure.

22 'Pro his nos habemus luxuriam atque ava-
ritiam, publice egestatem, privatim opulentiam;
laudamus divitias, sequimur inertiam; inter
bonos et malos discrimen nullum; omnia virtutis praemia ambitio possidet. 23 Neque mirum;
ubi vos separatim sibi quisque consilium capitis,
ubi domi voluptatibus, hic pecuniae aut gratiae
servitis, eo fit ut impetus fiat in vacuam rem
publicam.

24 'Sed ego haec omitto. Coniuravere nobili-
ssumi cives patriam incendere; Gallorum gen-
tem infestissumam nomini Romano ad bellum
arcessunt; dux hostium cum exercitu supra caput
est: 25 vos cunctamini etiam nunc et dubitatis
quid intra moenia deprensis hostibus faciatis?

26 'Misereamini censeo—deliquere homines
adulescentuli per ambitionem—atque etiam ar-
matos dimittatis. 27 Ne ista vobis mansuetudo
et misericordia, si illi arma ceperint, in miseriam
convortat.

28 'Scilicet res ipsa aspera est, sed vos non
timetis eam. Immo vero maxume; sed inertia et
mollitia animi alius alium expectantes cunctamini,

"Instead of these, we have luxury and greed, public poverty and immense private wealth. We celebrate being rich, we pursue idleness. Between good and bad men there is no distinction: ambition gets hold of all the prizes for merit. It's no surprise. When each of you thinks only of his own interests, when in private life you are enslaved to pleasures, here in the Senate to money or influence—that is how an assault is made on a defenseless Republic.

"But I let that pass. Citizens of the highest nobility have conspired to burn the fatherland. They have called to war the Gauls, a people utterly hostile to the name of Rome. The leader of the enemy with his army hangs over our heads. And you still waver and hesitate over what to do with an enemy caught in the city?

"Go ahead, I tell you, take pity: young men were led astray by ambition. Go ahead, release the armed men too. That mildness and mercy of yours would, if they take up arms, most likely turn into misery for yourselves.

"Doubtless this is a desperate situation, but you do not fear it. Actually, your fear is very great. But through inaction and weakness of will, you delay, each waiting for the other to act,

videlicet dis inmortalibus confisi, qui hanc rem publicam saepe in maxumis periculis ser- vavere. 29 Non votis neque suppliciis muliebri- bus auxilia deorum parantur: vigilando, agendo, bene consulundo prospere omnia cedunt. Vbi socordiae tete atque ignaviae tradideris, nequi- quam deos inplores; irati infestique sunt.

30 'Apud maiores nostros A. Manlius Tor- quatus bello Gallico filium suum, quod is con- tra imperium in hostem pugnaverat, necari ius- sit, 31 atque ille egregius adulescens inmoderatae fortitudinis morte poenas dedit: vos de crude- lissumis parricidis quid statuatis cunctamini? Videlicet cetera vita eorum huic sceleri ob- stat. 32 Verum parcite dignitati Lentuli, si ipse pudicitiae, si famae suae, si dis aut hominibus umquam ullis pepercit. 33 Ignoscite Cethegi adulescentiae, nisi iterum patriae bellum fecit. 34 Nam quid ego de Statilio, Gabinio, Caepario loquar? Quibus si quicquam umquam pensi fuis- set, non ea consilia de re publica habuissent.

apparently relying on the immortal gods, who often saved this Republic in its greatest moments of peril. Not by vows or by womanish prayers is the help of the gods gained. It is by vigilance, action, and good counsel that success comes. When you surrender to sluggishness and sloth, you will appeal to the gods in vain; they are angry and aggrieved.

"In our ancestors' day, during the war against the Gauls, Aulus Manlius Torquatus ordered his son killed for having fought the enemy against orders, and that upstanding young man paid with his life for his boundless courage. Now you are hesitating over what judgment to pass on the most ruthless traitors? Of course, you say, the rest of their lives are at odds with this crime. All right then, show respect for the authority of Lentulus—if he ever showed respect for his chastity and for his reputation and for any gods or men. Pardon the youth of Cethegus—if he has not for a second time made war on the fatherland. But what am I to say about Gabinius, Statilius, and Caeparius? If they ever had any scruples, they would not have harbored such designs against the Republic.

35 'Postremo, patres conscripti, si mehercule peccato locus esset, facile paterer vos ipsa re corrigi, quoniam verba contemnitis. Sed undique circumventi sumus; Catilina cum exercitu faucibus urget; alii intra moenia atque in sinu urbis sunt hostes, neque parari neque consuli quicquam potest occulte; quo magis properandum est.

36 'Quare ego ita censeo: cum nefario consilio sceleratorum civium res publica in maxuma pericula venerit, eique indicio T. Volturci et legatorum Allobrogum convicti confessique sint caedem, incendia aliaque se foeda atque crudelia facinora in civis patriamque paravisse, de confessis, sicuti de manufestis rerum capitalium, more maiorum supplicium sumundum.'

"Last of all, Senate Fathers, if there were room for error, by Hercules, I would gladly let your experience of it set you right, since you do not value words. But we are surrounded on all sides. Catiline and his army press at our throats; there are other enemies within the walls and even in the heart of the city; no preparation, no plan can be made without their knowledge. So all the more we must hurry.

"Therefore, this is my proposal. Since a wicked plan of criminal citizens has landed the Republic in the greatest peril, and since, through the testimony of Titus Volturcius and the Allobrogian envoys, those men have been proven guilty and confessed that they have planned murder, arson, and other cruel and horrible outrages against their fellow citizens and the fatherland, I propose that punishment according to the custom of our ancestors be inflicted on those who have confessed, as though they had been caught in the act of committing capital offenses."

53 Postquam Cato adsedit, consulares omnes itemque senatus magna pars sententiam eius laudant, virtutem animi ad caelum ferunt, alii alios increpantes timidos vocant. Cato clarus atque magnus habetur; senati decretum fit, sicuti ille censuerat.

2 Sed mihi multa legenti, multa audienti quae populus Romanus domi militiaeque, mari atque terra praeclara facinora fecit, forte lubuit adtendere quae res maxume tanta negotia sustinuisset. 3 Sciebam saepenumero parva manu cum magnis legionibus hostium contendisse; cognoveram parvis copiis bella gesta cum opulentis regibus; ad hoc saepe fortunae violentiam toleravisse, facundia Graecos, gloria belli Gallos ante Romanos fuisse.

4 Ac mihi multa agitanti constabat paucorum civium egregiam virtutem cuncta patravisse,

Two Men of Extraordinary Excellence [53–54]

After Cato sat down, all of the former consuls as well as a large majority of the Senate commended his proposal, praised to the skies his strength of character, and rebuked one another as cowards. Cato was looked upon as noble and great, and a decree of the Senate was passed as he had advised.

Reading and listening about the many splendid deeds that the Roman People have done at home and on campaign, by land and by sea, a desire came over me to examine what it was in particular that allowed such great undertakings. I knew that many times the Roman People had, with a small band of men, fought against the great armies of their enemies. I had learned that, with few resources, they had waged war against opulent kings; also, that they had often endured violent blows of Fortune; that the Romans were inferior to the Greeks in eloquence, to the Gauls in military renown.

As I turned over many points in my mind, it started to become evident that it was the remarkable excellence of a few citizens that made

eoque factum uti divitias paupertas, multitudinem paucitas superaret. 5 Sed postquam luxu
atque desidia civitas corrupta est, rursus res publica magnitudine sui imperatorum atque magistratuum vitia sustentabat ac, sicuti <esset>
effeta par[en]tu[m], multis tempestatibus haud
sane quisquam Romae virtute magnus fuit.

6 Sed memoria mea ingenti virtute, divorsis
moribus fuere viri duo, M. Cato et C. Caesar.
Quos quoniam res obtulerat, silentio praeterire
non fuit consilium quin utriusque naturam et
mores, quantum ingenio possum, aperirem.

54 Igitur eis genus, aetas, eloquentia prope ae-
qualia fuere; magnitudo animi par, item gloria,
sed alia alii. 2 Caesar beneficiis ac munificentia
magnus habebatur, integritate vitae Cato. Ille
mansuetudine et misericordia clarus factus, huic
severitas dignitatem addiderat. 3 Caesar dando,
sublevando, ignoscendo, Cato nihil largiundo

everything possible. This was why poverty overcame wealth, a handful of people a large number. But after the citizenry was corrupted by extravagance and inactivity, it was, by contrast, through its great size that the Republic withstood the faults of its generals and magistrates. As if worn out from giving birth, for many stretches of time Rome went without producing a single man distinguished by excellence.

Yet in my own time, there were two men of extraordinary excellence, though different characters: Marcus Cato and Gaius Caesar. And since they have appeared in my story, I am resolved not to pass over them in silence but to describe, to the extent of my ability, the nature and character of each.

In birth, years, and eloquence they were more or less equal. In greatness of soul they were alike, and glory too—but their glory was for different things. Caesar was regarded as great for his acts of kindness and generosity, Cato for the integrity of his life. The former gained distinction for his mildness and mercy, while the latter's prestige was enhanced by his austerity. Caesar won glory by giving, by supporting, by pardoning,

gloriam adeptus est. In altero miseris perfugium erat, in altero malis pernicies. Illius facilitas, huius constantia laudabatur. 4 Postremo Caesar in animum induxerat laborare, vigilare; negotiis amicorum intentus sua neglegere, nihil denegare quod dono dignum esset; sibi magnum imperium, exercitum, bellum novom exoptabat ubi virtus enitescere posset. 5 At Catoni studium modestiae, decoris, sed maxume severitatis erat; 6 non divitiis cum divite neque factione cum factioso, sed cum strenuo virtute, cum modesto pudore, cum innocente abstinentia certabat. Esse quam videri bonus malebat; ita, quo minus petebat gloriam, eo magis illum sequebatur.

55 Postquam, ut dixi, senatus in Catonis sententiam discessit, consul optumum factu ratus noctem quae instabat antecapere, ne quid eo spatio novaretur, triumviros quae [ad] supplicium

Cato by never being lavish. In one there was a refuge for the wretched, in the other the ruin of the wicked. The first was celebrated for his graciousness, the second for his steadfastness. Finally, Caesar made it his resolve to work hard and be up at all hours; attentive to his friends' problems, he neglected his own and denied nothing that was worth giving; for himself, he yearned for a great command, an army, a new war where his excellence could shine. But Cato's desire was for self-restraint, moral dignity, and austerity above all. He did not compete with the rich man in riches, nor in plotting with the plotter, but with the strong man in courage, with the restrained man in propriety, with the pure man in self-denial. He preferred to be honorable rather than to seem it—so much so that, the less he sought glory, the more it followed him.

The Execution of the Conspirators in Rome [55]

After the Senate voted for Cato's proposal, as I have mentioned, the consul, thinking it best to anticipate looming nightfall so that there would be no disturbance during that time, ordered the

postulabat parare iubet. 2 Ipse, praesidiis dispositis, Lentulum in carcerem deducit; 3 idem fit ceteris per praetores.

Est in carcere locus, quod Tullianum appellatur, ubi paululum ascenderis ad laevam, circiter duodecim pedes humi depressus. 4 Eum muniunt undique parietes atque insuper camera lapideis fornicibus iuncta; sed incultu, tenebris, odore foeda atque terribilis eius facies est. 5 In eum locum postquam demissus est Lentulus, vindices rerum capitalium, quibus praeceptum erat, laqueo gulam fregere. 6 Ita ille patricius ex gente clarissuma Corneliorum, qui consulare imperium Romae habuerat, dignum moribus factisque suis exitium vitae invenit. De Cethego, Statilio, Gabinio, Caepario eodem modo supplicium sumptum est.

56 Dum ea Romae geruntur, Catilina, ex omni copia quam et ipse adduxerat et Manlius habuerat, duas legiones instituit; cohortis pro

Commission of Three to prepare what the punishment required.[47] He himself, after deploying
guards, brought Lentulus to the prison.[48] The
same was done for the others by the praetors.

There is a place in the prison, called the Tullianum, which after you go up a little bit to the
left is sunken about twelve feet underground. It
is fortified with walls on all sides and overhead
by a vaulted roof made of stone arches; but
through neglect, gloom, and stench it had a foul
and frightening appearance. After Lentulus was
lowered down into this place, the executioners
to whom the order had been given broke his
neck with a noose. And so that patrician, a member of the illustrious family of the Cornelii
who had held the rank of consul at Rome, met
with an end to his life that was worthy of his
character and conduct. On Cethegus, Statilius,
Gabinius, and Caeparius punishment was inflicted in the same way.

Catiline on the Run [56–57.4]

While these events were happening at Rome,
Catiline formed two legions from all of the
forces that he had brought himself and that had

numero militum complet. 2 Deinde, ut quisque voluntarius aut ex sociis in castra venerat, aequaliter distribuerat ac brevi spatio legiones numero hominum expleverat, cum initio non amplius duobus milibus habuisset. 3 Sed ex omni copia circiter pars quarta erat militaribus armis instructa; ceteri, ut quemque casus armaverat, sparos aut lanceas, alii praeacutas sudis portare.

4 Sed postquam Antonius cum exercitu adventabat, Catilina per montis iter facere, modo ad urbem, modo in Galliam vorsus castra movere, hostibus occasionem pugnandi non dare; sperabat propediem magnas copias sese habiturum, si Romae socii incepta patravissent. 5 Interea servitia repudiabat, cuius initio ad eum magnae copiae concurrebant, opibus coniurationis fretus, simul alienum suis rationibus existumans videri causam civium cum servis fugitivis communicavisse.

been in the possession of Manlius. The strength of the cohorts was based on the number of soldiers at Catiline's disposal. Then, whenever new volunteers or one of the allies joined the camp, he distributed them evenly, and in a brief space of time he had filled out the legions with the standard number of men, even though initially he had had no more than two thousand.[49] Yet out of his entire force only around one-quarter were equipped with military weapons. The rest bore hunting spears or lances, some very sharp sticks—whatever chance armed them with.

But after Antonius started to draw near with his army, Catiline marched through the mountains, moved his camp at one time toward Rome and another toward Gaul, and gave the enemy no opportunity to fight. He was hoping that, any day now, he would have a large army, if his allies in Rome carried out their plans. Meanwhile, he kept refusing to accept slaves, great numbers of whom were at first flocking to him. He was confident in the resources of the conspiracy and also thought it not in keeping with his interests to seem to have joined the cause of citizens with fugitive slaves.

57 Sed postquam in castra nuntius pervenit Romae coniurationem patefactam, de Lentulo et Cethego ceterisque quos supra memoravi supplicium sumptum, plerique, quos ad bellum spes rapinarum aut novarum rerum studium inlexerat, dilabuntur; relicuos Catilina per montis asperos magnis itineribus in agrum Pistoriensem abducit, eo consilio uti per tramites occulte perfugeret in Galliam Transalpinam.

2 At Q. Metellus Celer cum tribus legionibus in agro Piceno praesidebat, ex difficultate rerum eadem illa existumans quae supra diximus Catilinam agitare. 3 Igitur, ubi iter eius ex perfugis cognovit, castra propere movit ac sub ipsis radicibus montium consedit, qua illi descensus erat in Galliam properanti. 4 Neque tamen Antonius procul aberat, utpote qui magno exercitu locis aequioribus expeditos in fuga sequeretur.

But after news reached the camp that at Rome the conspiracy had been brought to light and punishment had been inflicted on Lentulus, Cethegus, and the others I mentioned above, a great number of conspirators who had been drawn to war by hope of plundering or eagerness for revolution now slipped away. Catiline withdrew the rest by forced marches over rugged mountains to the region around Pistoria. His plan was to escape undetected on footpaths to Transalpine Gaul.[50]

But Quintus Metellus Celer with his three legions was standing watch in the territory of Picenum, judging that the difficulty of Catiline's position would lead him to form exactly the plans I have just mentioned. When Celer learned Catiline's route from the deserters, he swiftly broke camp and took up a position right at the foot of the mountains where Catiline would need to descend as he hurried to Gaul. Nor was Antonius far away, when one considers that with his large army he was pursuing, on more level ground, lightly equipped men in flight.

5 Sed Catilina, postquam videt montibus atque copiis hostium sese clausum, in urbe res advorsas, neque fugae neque praesidi ullam spem, optumum factu ratus in tali re fortunam belli temptare, statuit cum Antonio quam primum confligere. 6 Itaque, contione advocata, huiusce modi orationem habuit.

58 'Compertum ego habeo, milites, verba virtutem non addere, neque ex ignavo strenuum neque fortem ex timido exercitum oratione imperatoris fieri. 2 Quanta cuiusque animo audacia natura aut moribus inest, tanta in bello patere solet. Quem neque gloria neque pericula excitant, nequiquam hortere: timor animi auribus officit. 3 Sed ego vos quo pauca monerem advocavi, simul uti causam mei consili aperirem.

4 'Scitis equidem, milites, socordia atque ignavia Lentuli quantam ipsi nobisque cladem attulerit, quoque modo, dum ex urbe praesidia opperior, in Galliam proficisci nequiverim.

The Final Battle [57.5–61]

Catiline, after he saw that he was hemmed in by the mountains and the enemy army, that the situation in Rome was hostile, and that there was no hope of escape or reinforcement, judged it best in such circumstances to try the fortune of war and resolved on a clash with Antonius as soon as possible. He therefore called an assembly and gave a speech like this.

"I have discovered, soldiers, that words do not increase courage, nor does an army go from being sluggish to energetic, timid to brave, because of a speech from their commander. However much boldness there is in each man's heart, whether inborn or from upbringing, is usually revealed in war. The man whom neither glory nor dangers arouse you would urge on in vain; the fear in his soul blocks his ears. Still, I have gathered you together to remind you of a few things and also explain the reasoning behind my plan.

"You are aware, soldiers, what a great disaster Lentulus's laziness and lack of energy brought on himself and on us and how, while I was awaiting reinforcements from the city, I

5 Nunc vero quo loco res nostrae sint iuxta mecum omnes intellegitis. 6 Exercitus hostium duo, unus ab urbe, alter a Gallia obstant. Diutius in his locis esse, si maxume animus ferat, frumenti atque aliarum rerum egestas prohibet. 7 Quocumque ire placet, ferro iter aperiundum est.

8 'Quapropter vos moneo uti forti atque parato animo sitis et, cum proelium inibitis, memineritis vos divitias, decus, gloriam, praeterea libertatem atque patriam in dextris vostris portare. 9 Si vincimus, omnia nobis tuta erunt: commeatus abunde, municipia atque coloniae patebunt. 10 Si metu cesserimus, eadem illa advorsa fient. Neque locus neque amicus quisquam teget quem arma non texerint.

11 'Praeterea, milites, non eadem nobis et illis necessitudo inpendet. Nos pro patria, pro libertate, pro vita certamus; illis supervacuaneum est pugnare pro potentia paucorum. 12 Quo audacius adgredimini memores pristinae virtutis.

13 'Licuit vobis cum summa turpitudine in exilio aetatem agere; potuistis nonnulli Romae,

could not set out for Gaul. Where our situation now stands you all understand just as well as I do. Two armies of the enemy stand in our way, one from Rome, the other from Gaul. Lack of grain and other supplies forbids us to remain longer here, even if we were particularly inclined to. Wherever we resolve to go, the way must be opened by the sword.

"Therefore, I urge you to be brave and determined in spirit. When you join battle, remember that you hold in your own hands wealth, honor, glory, even freedom and your fatherland. If we win, all will be safe for us. Supplies will abound. Towns and colonies will be thrown open. If we yield out of fear, those same places will be hostile. No place, no friend will protect a man whose own arms have not protected him.

"Furthermore, soldiers, the same necessity does not press upon us as upon them. We are engaged in a struggle for our fatherland, for our freedom, for our lives. For them it serves no purpose to fight for the power of a few. Therefore, make your attack more boldly, mindful of your former worth.

"You might have passed your life in exile with the greatest dishonor. Some of you could have

amissis bonis, alienas opes expectare. 14 Quia illa foeda atque intoleranda viris videbantur, haec sequi decrevistis. 15 Si haec relinquere voltis, audacia opus est; nemo nisi victor pace bellum mutavit. 16 Nam in fuga salutem sperare, cum arma quibus corpus tegitur ab hostibus avorteris, ea vero dementia est. 17 Semper in proelio eis maxumum est periculum qui maxume timent; audacia pro muro habetur.

18 'Cum vos considero, milites, et cum facta vostra aestumo, magna me spes victoriae tenet. 19 Animus, aetas, virtus vostra me hortantur, praeterea necessitudo, quae etiam timidos fortis facit. 20 Nam multitudo hostium ne circumvenire queat prohibent angustiae loci. 21 Quod si virtuti vostrae fortuna inviderit, cavete inulti animam amittatis, neu capti potius sicuti pecora trucidemini quam virorum more pugnantes cruentam atque luctuosam victoriam hostibus relinquatis.'

59 Haec ubi dixit, paululum commoratus, signa canere iubet atque instructos ordines in

hoped for help from others in Rome, after you lost your property. Since that seemed dishonorable and unbearable to real men, you decided to pursue the present course of action. If you wish to abandon it, boldness is needed; no one except a conqueror has exchanged war for peace. To hope for deliverance in flight, when you have turned the arms that protect your body away from the enemy, is pure madness. In battle, danger is always greatest for those who are the most afraid; boldness is as good as a rampart.

"When I look upon you, soldiers, and when I weigh your deeds, great hope of victory takes hold of me. Your spirit, your youth, your courage urge me on—also necessity, which makes even fearful men brave. The enemy, despite its great number, cannot encircle us; the narrow defile prevents that. But if Fortune frowns on your courage, take care not to give up your life unavenged. Do not let yourself be captured and slaughtered like cattle. Fight like men and leave the enemy with a bloody and sorrowful victory."

Having said this, after delaying a short while he had the trumpet sounded and marched the troops, arrayed in battle formation, to level

locum aequom deducit. Dein, remotis omnium
equis quo militibus exaequato periculo animus
amplior esset, ipse pedes exercitum pro loco
atque copiis instruit. 2 Nam, uti planities erat
inter sinistros montis et ab dextra rupe—
aspera—, octo cohortis in fronte constituit,
relicuarum signa in subsidio artius conlocat.
3 Ab eis centuriones, omnis lectos et evoca-
tos, praeterea ex gregariis militibus optumum
quemque armatum in primam aciem subducit.
C. Manlium in dextra, Faesulanum quendam
in sinistra parte curare iubet; ipse cum liber-
tis et calonibus propter aquilam adsistit quam
bello Cimbrico C. Marius in exercitu habuisse
dicebatur.

4 At ex altera parte C. Antonius, pedibus
aeger, quod proelio adesse nequibat, M. Petreio
legato exercitum permittit. 5 Ille cohortis vete-
ranas, quas tumultus causa conscripserat, in
fronte, post eas ceterum exercitum in subsidiis
locat. Ipse equo circumiens unum quemque

ground. Then, after having everyone's horses removed so that the soldier's courage would be greater with the danger made equal for all, on foot himself, he arranged his troops according to the terrain and the numbers he had. Because the plain was between mountains on the left and a rugged rock face on the right, he stationed eight cohorts in front and placed the rest of his divisions, more tightly packed, in reserve. From them, he drew off into the front line the centurions—all carefully chosen men and veterans—as well as those best armed from the rank and file.[51] He ordered Gaius Manlius to take charge on the right, a certain man from Faesulae on the left. Catiline himself, along with his freedmen and camp-servants, took a position next to the eagle that Gaius Marius was said to have had in his army during the war against the Cimbri.[52]

On the other side, because Gaius Antonius, ill with gout, could not be present at the battle, he entrusted the army to his officer Marcus Petreius. Petreius positioned the cohorts of veterans that he had enrolled on account of the state of emergency in front, and behind them the rest of the army as reserves. He himself went around

nominans appellat, hortatur, rogat ut meminerint se contra latrones inermos pro patria, pro liberis, pro aris atque focis suis certare. 6 Homo militaris, quod amplius annos triginta tribunus aut praefectus aut legatus aut praetor cum magna gloria in exercitu fuerat, plerosque ipsos factaque eorum fortia noverat. Ea commemorando militum animos accendebat.

60 Sed ubi, omnibus rebus exploratis, Petreius tuba signum dat, cohortis paulatim incedere iubet; idem facit hostium exercitus. 2 Postquam eo ventum est unde a ferentariis proelium committi posset, maxumo clamore cum infestis signis concurrunt; pila omittunt; gladiis res geritur. 3 Veterani pristinae virtutis memores comminus acriter instare; illi haud timidi resistunt; maxuma vi certatur.

4 Interea Catilina cum expeditis in prima acie vorsari, laborantibus succurrere, integros pro

on his horse and, naming each soldier, called out to them, made appeals to them, and encouraged them to remember that they were fighting against unarmed brigands on behalf of their fatherland, their children, and their hearths and altars. An experienced soldier—for more than thirty years he had served in the army with great distinction as a tribune, prefect, officer, or commander—he knew most of the men personally and their courageous deeds. By recalling those deeds, he inflamed the soldiers' spirits.

When, after inspecting everything, Petreius gave the signal with the trumpet, he ordered his cohorts to advance gradually. The enemy army did the same. After they drew near enough that combat could be initiated by the skirmishers, with a loud shout the hostile armies rushed at each other. Spears were discarded. The fight was with swords. The veterans, mindful of their former valor, fiercely pressed forward, battling hand-to-hand. Catiline's forces, without a trace of fear, resisted. It was a contest of the greatest fury.

Throughout it, Catiline was whirling about with the light-armed troops in the front line, running to help those struggling, calling on men

sauciis arcessere, omnia providere, multum ipse pugnare, saepe hostem ferire; strenui militis et boni imperatoris officia simul exsequebatur.

5 Petreius, ubi videt Catilinam, contra ac ratus erat, magna vi tendere, cohortem praetoriam in medios hostis inducit eosque perturbatos atque alios alibi resistentis interficit; deinde utrimque ex lateribus ceteros adgreditur. 6 Manlius et Faesulanus in primis pugnantes cadunt. 7 <Catilina>, postquam fusas copias seque cum paucis relicuom videt, memor generis atque pristinae suae dignitatis in confertissumos hostis incurrit ibique pugnans confoditur.

61 Sed, confecto proelio, tum vero cerneres quanta audacia quantaque animi vis fuisset in exercitu Catilinae 2 Nam fere quem quisque vivos pugnando locum ceperat, eum, amissa anima, corpore tegebat. 3 Pauci autem, quos medios cohors praetoria disiecerat, paulo divorsius, sed omnes tamen advorsis volneribus

to take the place of the wounded, attending to everything, fighting a great deal himself, hitting the enemy often. He was performing the duties of an active soldier and a good commander at the same time.

When Petreius, contrary to what he expected, saw Catiline exerting himself with great force, Petreius led his own bodyguard against the enemy's center, threw them into confusion, and killed them as well as others in other places as they tried to resist. He then attacked the rest of the army on both flanks. Manlius and the officer from Faesulae were among the first to fall fighting. After Catiline saw that his army was scattered and he was left with just a few men, mindful of his birth and his former prestige, he dashed against the enemy where they were most crowded together and while fighting there was struck down.

After the battle was finished, the boldness and determination in Catiline's army could truly be seen. Nearly all the dead covered with their bodies the ground where they had taken their stand fighting while still alive. A few in the middle, however, scattered by Petreius's guard, were a little farther away, but still, all had fallen

conciderant. 4 Catilina vero longe a suis inter hostium cadavera repertus est, paululum etiam spirans ferociamque animi quam habuerat vivos in voltu retinens. 5 Postremo ex omni copia neque in proelio neque in fuga quisquam civis ingenuos captus est: 6 ita cuncti suae hostiumque vitae iuxta pepercerant.

7 Neque tamen exercitus populi Romani laetam aut incruentam victoriam adeptus erat; nam strenuissimus quisque aut occiderat in proelio aut graviter volneratus discesserat. 8 Multi autem, qui e castris visundi aut spoliandi gratia processerant, volventes hostilia cadavera amicum alii, pars hospitem aut cognatum reperiebant; fuere item qui inimicos suos cognoscerent. 9 Ita varie per omnem exercitum laetitia maeror, luctus, atque gaudia agitabantur.

with wounds in front. Catiline, though, was found far from his own men among the corpses of the enemy, still breathing a little and preserving on his face the ferocity of spirit he had had while living. Out of the whole army, no freeborn citizen of Rome was captured in battle or in flight. Everyone had spared their own lives exactly as much as the enemy's.

But it was no joyous or bloodless victory that the army of the Roman People had gained. All the finest either fell in battle or withdrew gravely wounded. And many, having come from the camp to look around or plunder, as they turned over the enemy corpses found a friend here, a host or kinsman there. There were some, too, who recognized their personal enemies. So throughout the whole army feelings of gladness and sorrow, mourning and rejoicing, were variously aroused.

ACKNOWLEDGMENTS

Once again, Rob Tempio at Princeton University Press had the idea for this book, and I thank him for asking me to develop it in 2018. As I brought this translation to completion in January 2021, Rob's insight that Sallust had commentary relevant to our own times seemed ever cannier.

I also owe an enormous debt to Danny O'Sullivan, a 2020 graduate of Georgetown College. Over the summer of 2020 he worked through a first draft of the translation with me, suggesting countless improvements. His keen grasp of Latin style and metaphor was an inspiration. Danny also enriched the introduction to this book, especially the discussion of Thucydides.

Three readers for Princeton University Press provided helpful evaluations, one of which was especially detailed and saved me from a number of mistakes. I have silently incorporated the

readers' corrections and many of their suggestions and warmly thank all three of them. Copyeditor Cynthia Buck brought more clarity throughout.

I have tried to render Sallust's Latin into an easy-to-read translation while still capturing something of its pungency. In doing so, I relied a lot on previous translations and editions of *The War against Catiline*, especially those of John Selby Watson (1870); Minard Sturgus (rev. 1872); J. C. Rolfe (rev. 1931); Alfred Ernout (rev. 1989 by Joseph Hellegouarc'h); A. J. Woodman (2007); and John T. Ramsey (2007); and on Ramsey's thorough revision of Rolfe's Loeb (2013). My Latin text draws on these works as well as the editions of Alfons Kurfess (1957) and L. D. Reynolds (1991). Woodman's and Ramsey's work has been particularly helpful as well as stimulating, and I thank them both for their help to me over the years.

NOTES

Introduction

1. Richard Hofstadter, *The Paranoid Style in American Politics and Other Essays* (New York: Vintage, 1965), 3.

2. Ibid., 21.

3. Gordon S. Wood, "Conspiracy and the Paranoid Style: Causality and Deceit in the Eighteenth Century," *William and Mary Quarterly* 39, no. 3 (1982): 402–41; reprinted in Wood, *The Idea of America: Reflections on the Birth of the United States* (New York: Penguin Press, 2011), 81–123. For more similarly less pejorative perspectives, see Victoria E. Pagán, *Conspiracy Theory in Latin Literature* (Austin: University of Texas Press, 2012).

4. Hofstadter, *The Paranoid Style in American Politics*, 29.

5. For Sallust's influence on John Adams, see James M. Farrell, "New England's Cicero: John Adams and the Rhetoric of Conspiracy," *Proceedings of the Massachusetts Historical Society* 104 (1992): 55–72. Catiline's prominence in the political rhetoric of the nascent United States is highlighted throughout

Thomas E. Ricks, *First Principles: What America's Founders Learned from the Greeks and Romans and How That Shaped Our Country* (New York: HarperCollins, 2020).

6. Suetonius, *Domitian* 20.

7. See, for example, Barbara Levick, *Catiline* (London: Bloomsbury, 2015), esp. 45–57. Some particularly skeptical scholars have even suggested that Catiline only decided to revolt after his flight from Rome in early November 63; see, for example, Robin Seager, "Iusta Catilinae," *Historia* 22 (1973): 240–48.

8. John T. Ramsey, "The Date of the Consular Elections in 63 and the Inception of Catiline's Conspiracy," *Harvard Studies in Classical Philology* 110 (2020): 213–69, esp. 251–54.

9. Cassius Dio, *Roman History* 43.9.2–3.

10. According to the late antique writer Jerome (*Against Jovinianus* 1.48), Cicero's ex-wife Terentia subsequently married Sallust. Jerome's testimony is problematic. It has been suggested that it was Cicero's second wife, Publilia, whom Sallust married. See Ronald Syme, "Sallust's Wife," *Classical Quarterly* 28 (1978): 292–95.

11. Thucydides, *History* 3.82.8.

12. See especially Sallust's *War against Jugurtha* 41.2–3.

13. For a discussion of this approach, see Josiah Osgood, *Rome and the Making of a World State, 150 BCE–20 CE* (Cambridge: Cambridge University Press, 2018), 1–9.

14. See, for example, Ronald Syme, *Sallust* (Berkeley: University of California Press, 1964), 83–102.
15. But for an important alternative view of events from 66 to 64, see A. J. Woodman, "Sallust and Catiline: Conspiracy Theories," *Historia* 70 (2021): 55–68. Also less skeptical of Sallust is A. M. Stone, "Was Sallust a Liar? A Problem in Modern History," in *Ancient History in a Modern University: Early Christianity, Late Antiquity, and Beyond*, edited by T. W. Hillard et al. (Grand Rapids, MI: Eerdmans, 1998), 230–43.
16. Quoted in Joseph J. Ellis, *Founding Brothers: The Revolutionary Generation* (New York: Knopf, 2000), 42. My discussion is indebted to Ellis's account.
17. Ibid.
18. On the other hand, a conspiracy might be launched to save a republic from tyranny, as the assassins of Caesar said they were doing in 44 BC.
19. On Sallust's *War against Catiline* as a tribute to Ciceronian leadership, see the important paper by A. M. Stone, "Tribute to a Statesman: Cicero and Sallust," *Antichthon* 33 (1999): 48–76.

The War against Catiline

1. Sallust refers here to the senators, who in his own day were still collectively known as "the Fathers."
2. These officers eventually came to be known as consuls.

3. After the fall of Carthage in the Third Punic War (149–146 BC), the Romans razed the ancient city.

4. Sallust refers to Sulla's takeover of the city of Rome in 82 and the ensuing proscriptions (described in the introduction).

5. Rich Romans built luxury villas perched on cliffs or stretched on piers across the sea, seemingly in defiance of nature.

6. Cicero claims (for example, in *Against Catiline* 2.8) that Catiline had sex with the young men he associated with, both penetrating them and letting himself be penetrated, the latter being particularly scandalous for a freeborn Roman man.

7. The identity of the "girl of noble birth" is unknown, but the Vestal Virgin was Fabia, the half-sister of Cicero's wife Terentia.

8. As discussed in the introduction, modern historians have been skeptical of the plans that Sallust ascribes to Sallust for the years 65 and 64.

9. Crassus was among the wealthiest and most powerful senators of his day. He resented how Pompey usurped much of the credit for putting down the uprising led by the gladiator Spartacus in the late 70s.

10. As Sallust may hint here, there were rival versions of this "first Catilinarian conspiracy." But see Woodman, "Sallust and Catiline: Conspiracy Theories," which argues that Sallust actually wrote "as briefly as I can."

11. The fasces, bundles of wooden rods bound by straps, were the symbols of the consuls' power.

12. Piso's exact title, given by Sallust, was "propraetorian quaestor." This means that though he was only of quaestorian rank, he had the authority of a praetor.

13. Like Thucydides, Sallust typically uses the expression "like this" to mark speeches he is giving in his own words.

14. Gaius Antonius did end up winning a consulship for 63 along with Cicero.

15. A former officer of Sulla's granted land in Faesulae (modern Fiesole, just outside Florence), Manlius headed up a group of disgruntled veterans and victims of Sulla's confiscations there.

16. Later referred to by Sallust as the wife of Decimus Iunius Brutus, the consul of 77, the intriguing Sempronia is otherwise unknown.

17. Sallust is referring to the elections in 63 for the magistracies of 62.

18. Early in the year 63, Cicero arranged for the province he would govern after his consulship (Macedonia) to be transferred to Antonius.

19. The election was in late September, as demonstrated by Ramsey, "The Date of the Consular Elections." Cicero wore a well-polished breastplate for the occasion and made sure to let his tunic slip so that voters would see it—and think they were in peril from Catiline.

20. This is the so-called ultimate decree of the Senate, first passed in the year 121. It was a subject of great controversy, and many would have disputed Sallust's subsequent explanation.

21. Capua, in southern Italy, was famous for its gladiatorial schools; it was here that Spartacus's rebellion broke out. Apulia (modern Puglia) was also known for slave uprisings, especially among the many herdsmen there.

22. These were large sums of money; a soldier's base pay was perhaps as little as 450 sesterces per annum.

23. The law dealt with violence against individuals or the state; Paullus was never able to complete the prosecution because Catiline fled Rome first.

24. This is Cicero's so-called First Catilinarian, delivered November 7 or 8.

25. While Cicero was born in the little town of Arpinum, about sixty miles southeast of Rome in the Volscian mountains, he was hardly a foreigner, as Catiline's sneer suggested; Cicero's family had enjoyed citizenship for generations.

26. It was common practice to stop the not-infrequent fires that broke out in the city of Rome by destroying whole blocks of buildings.

27. As before, the phrase "like this" marks that the message is given in Sallust's words.

28. The envoys seem to be claiming that citizens in debt were being forced into slavery, contrary to Roman law. The claims of creditors were heard by one of the annually elected praetors.

29. At several points in the Republic's early history, tradition held, the plebeians withdrew to form an alternative government to put pressure on those in power.

30. Catulus, consul in 78, was de facto leader of the nobles who dominated the Senate at this time. Note that Sallust does not introduce the letter with his usual "like this" but rather indicates that he is providing a "copy." The letter, which appears somewhat hastily written and has many words and phrases unattested elsewhere in Sallust, is likely to be authentic. See D. H. Berry, *Cicero's Catilinarians* (New York: Oxford University Press, 2020), 38–41.

31. On the restoration in 70 of the power of the tribunes of the plebs after curtailment by Sulla, see the introduction.

32. The reference is to Pompey, a figure of great suspicion in Sallust's writings.

33. The equestrian Gabinius Capito, mentioned earlier by Sallust in his list of conspirators, outranked the businessman Umbrenus, who, according to Cicero (*Against Catiline* 3.14), was an ex-slave.

34. Sallust perhaps slipped in writing that Bestia would act once Catiline had made it to Faesulae; the uprising was to begin when Catiline had brought his army to Rome. Alternatively, the manuscripts are in error.

35. The Mulvian Bridge over the Tiber River, just to the north of the heart of Rome, is most famous today

for the victory of the first Christian emperor, Constantine, over his rival Maxentius in AD 312.

36. Despite the Senate's passage of its emergency decree, responsibility for what Cicero did as magistrate would ultimately fall on him personally.

37. The Temple of Concord, an imposing building that overlooked the Forum, had been built centuries earlier to mark the end of a period of civil strife and had been rebuilt after the death of the popular champion Gaius Gracchus in 121—associations Cicero might have wished to evoke.

38. The great temple of Jupiter Optimus Maximus on the Capitoline had burned down in 83, the same year Sulla returned from the East and plunged Italy into fighting.

39. Especially to be noted in this list of senators who were to have custody over the conspirators is Gaius Julius Caesar, the future dictator.

40. Piso had served as governor of Gaul in 66–65 and was put on trial after his return. Caesar's defeat of the distinguished ex-consul Catulus in the election for pontifex maximus, chief priest of Rome, had happened earlier, in 63.

41. On the standard view, the debate on what to do about the conspirators took place on December 5, but for an argument that discussion began the day before, see A. J. Woodman, "Cicero and Sallust: Debating Death," *Histos* 15 (2021): 1–21.

42. In the Third Macedonian War (171–168), fought against Perseus, the last king of Macedon, the small

island of Rhodes aroused Rome's anger by suggesting that the Rhodians mediate the conflict.

43. Caesar refers to a law of the early second century that limited the right of magistrates to flog citizens.

44. After victory in the Peloponnesian War (431–404), the Spartans abolished the Athenian democracy and replaced it with an oligarchic board of thirty men who ruled for eight months.

45. Caesar refers to executions, following Sulla's victory, carried out just outside the walls of Rome in November 82, before the proscriptions began.

46. In later years, Cato was a dominant figure in the Senate, but in 63 he was still a relatively junior member of the body, having only held the quaestorship.

47. The Commission of Three were junior magistrates who, among other responsibilities, carried out executions.

48. The prison was a small building very close to the Forum, used for brief incarcerations and executions.

49. A legion was typically made up of ten cohorts with a little under five hundred men per cohort; thus, at first Catiline's units were only at about one-fifth of normal strength.

50. Catiline perhaps hoped, after crossing the Alps, to join up with the Allobroges, who in fact would rebel against Rome in 62.

51. Centurions were noncommissioned officers who commanded groups of around eighty men; they were the backbone of the Roman army.

52. The great general Marius, who saved Rome from an invasion of Germanic peoples, including the Cimbri, in the late second century, made it customary for each legion in the army to have a silver eagle as its standard. Catiline apparently used one of the eagles to rally his followers, almost as if it were a talisman. For him to stand by an eagle in battle showed great bravery.

FURTHER READING

The Catilinarian conspiracy inspired not one but two masterpieces of Latin literature. Along with Sallust's *War against Catiline*, we have Cicero's orations against Catiline, which can be read in the fine translation of D. H. Berry, *Cicero: Political Speeches* (Oxford: Oxford University Press, 2006). Berry has also written an excellent study, *Cicero's Catilinarians* (New York: Oxford University Press, 2020), which contains a superb account of the Catilinarian conspiracy and its later reception.

The best-documented recent study of Catiline is in French, Gianpaolo Urso's *Catilina: Le faux populiste* (Bordeaux: Ausonius Éditions, 2019). Briefer but also insightful is Barbara Levick, *Catiline* (London: Bloomsbury, 2015).

For those who wish to study the text in Latin, John T. Ramsey's *Sallust's Bellum Catilinae*, 2nd ed. (Oxford: Oxford University Press, 2007), is the indispensable starting point; I have

relied heavily on it. Also packed with useful information—and accessible to those without Latin—is Ramsey's thorough revision of the Loeb Classical Library edition of Sallust's *War with Catiline* and *War with Jugurtha* (Cambridge, MA: Harvard University Press, 2013). Those who want to read more Sallust should try his *War against Jugurtha*, available in the last volume, and also A. J. Woodman's excellent translation, *Catiline's War, The Jugurthine War, Histories* (London: Penguin, 2007).

A vivid evocation of the late Roman Republic is given by Tom Holland in *Rubicon: The Triumph and Tragedy of the Roman Republic* (New York: Doubleday, 2003). For a survey that integrates political, cultural, and social history, see my own *Rome and the Making of a World State, 150 BCE–20 CE* (Cambridge: Cambridge University Press, 2018).

The influence of Roman history and literature on the founding of the United States is discussed among others by Gordon Wood, *The Idea of America: Reflections on the Birth of the United States* (New York: Penguin Press, 2011), and Thomas E. Ricks, *First Principles: What America's Founders Learned from the Greeks*

and Romans and How That Shaped Our Country (New York: HarperCollins, 2020). Catiline's restless spirit is shown haunting the early United States again and again in Ricks's fine study.

Finally, I recommend two novels that are both entertaining and well informed: Steven Saylor's *Catilina's Riddle* (New York: St. Martin's Press, 1993), and Robert Harris's *Lustrum* (London: Arrow, 2010; published in the more paranoid United States as *Conspirata*).